AENEID
BOOK TWO

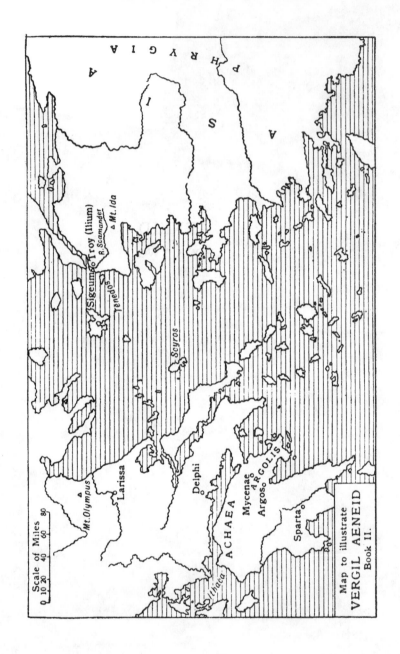

Map to illustrate
VERGIL AENEID
Book II.

VERGIL
AENEID II
THE SCOURGE OF ROME

EDITED WITH INTRODUCTION,
NOTES AND VOCABULARY
BY H.E. GOULD & J.L. WHITELEY

PUBLISHED BY BRISTOL CLASSICAL PRESS
GENERAL EDITOR: JOHN H. BETTS
(BY ARRANGEMENT WITH MACMILLAN & CO. LTD)

First published by Macmillan & Co. Ltd in 1943

This edition published in 1991 by
Bristol Classical Press
an imprint of
Gerald Duckworth & Co. Ltd
The Old Piano Factory
48 Hoxton Square, London N1 6PB

Reprinted 1992, 1994, 1995, 1996

A catalogue record for this book is available
from the British Library

ISBN 0-86292-056-6

Available in USA and Canada from:
Focus Information Group
PO Box 369
Newburyport
MA 01950

Printed in Great Britain by
Booksprint, Bristol

CONTENTS

LIST OF ILLUSTRATIONS

'ILLE SIMUL MANIBUS TENDIT DIVELLERE NODOS'

The serpents destroy Laocoon and his sons.
(Marble group in the Vatican.)

FOREWORD

THE present edition of Vergil's Aeneid II has been prepared on the same principles as previous volumes in the Modern School Classics Series. That is to say, the editors, believing that the annotated Classical texts of the past generation give too little practical assistance in translation, and yet have their commentaries overloaded with unnecessary information on points only remotely connected with the text, have sought to write notes of a type better suited to the requirements of the school boy or girl of to-day, who is quite likely to embark on the preparation of the School Certificate set books without having previously read any continuous Latin texts at all.

In such circumstances these pupils will need a great deal of help which in the spacious days of classical teaching fifty years ago they were considered not to require, and they will need moreover that such assistance should at first be given repeatedly, until each difficulty of construction becomes familiar.

The editors hope that, bearing in mind, as they

have throughout, the difficulties experienced by
present-day pupils in the study of a subject which
once received a much more generous share of the
time-table, they have done something, in the present
edition, to smooth their path.

H. E. G.

J. L. W.

WELLINGBOROUGH, 1942.

INTRODUCTION

Publius Vergilius Maro

VERGIL was born on October 15th in 70 B.C. at
Andes near Mantua in Cisalpine Gaul (the Lom-
bardy Plain). Andes is usually identified with
Pietole, which is about three miles from Mantua,
but, more recently, Professor Conway, supported by
Professor Rose, prefers a site not far from the modern
towns of Carpenedolo and Calvisano.[1]

The poet's family seems to have been of some local
importance, and his father, who owned and worked
a farm, was able to give his son the ancient equivalent of a university education. Vergil studied at
Cremona and Milan, and later went on to Rome to
complete his course in rhetoric and philosophy.

No doubt his father wished Vergil to make his
way, as Cicero had done, by his eloquence, first in
the law courts as a pleader, or barrister, and then in
politics by standing as a candidate for the various
magistracies which led to the consulship and a seat
in the senate. Vergil's temperament, however, for
he was shy, nervous and awkward in society, was

[1] Rose : *A Handbook of Latin Literature*, pp. 236–7.

unsuited to such a career, and, after one appearance before a jury, he decided to devote himself to philosophy and poetry.

Later he returned to his native district, where he began to write his first important work, the Eclogues or Bucolics, ten poems of a pastoral nature which made his reputation as a poet and gained the attention of Maecenas, who at this time was unofficial Minister for Home Affairs to Octavian, the heir of Julius Caesar, master of Italy, and destined shortly to become lord of the Greco-Roman world as the first Roman Emperor.

During this period, in 41 B.C., Vergil was one of the many small-holders who saw their farms ruthlessly confiscated and allotted to demobilised soldiers—a common event during those troubled years of civil war which preceded the collapse of the Roman Republic.

Fortunately, however, the fame of the Eclogues and his friendship with Maecenas made Vergil's position secure, and enabled him to devote the rest of his life to poetical composition, free from worry, at Naples and Nola in Campania.

Thus, in or about 37 B.C., Vergil began his second great work, the Georgics, a long poem in four books which describes the Roman methods of farming, the production of crops, of the vine and the olive, stockbreeding and bee-keeping. As we know from Vergil himself that he was asked to write on this subject by Maecenas, we may safely assume that his poem was intended to be propaganda for Octavian's (Augustus') new order in Italy and to reinforce the emperor's attempts to revive Roman religion, Roman agriculture, and the simple but hardy virtues which had made Rome great.

The two thousand odd lines of the poem were written very slowly,[1] and reveal the highest standard of pure craftsmanship yet reached in Latin poetry. Moreover, though his subject in this poem might seem unlikely to produce great poetry, Vergil found the theme so congenial to his nature that he overcame the many difficulties, and not only produced a practical handbook for farmers, but also wrote some of the noblest poetry in the Latin language.

Soon after the completion of the Georgics, Vergil, now 40 years of age, was quickly launched upon his greatest and most ambitious work, the writing of an epic (the Aeneid) which would not only rival Homer's Iliad and Odyssey, but also honour the imperial achievements of the Roman race, glorify the Roman character, and focus Roman feeling and national sentiment on Augustus as the man sent by destiny to bring peace, stability and prosperity to the

[1] From 37–30 B.C.

Greco-Roman world, for so many years torn by civil war, fear and uncertainty.

This epic poem occupied his whole attention for the remaining years of his life. In 19 B.C., after a voyage to the East, he fell ill and died on his return to Italy at Brundisium, before he had had time to revise his work—a task he had set himself for the next three years. He was so conscientious an artist that he seems to have been little satisfied with his work, for it is said that on his death-bed he gave instructions for the poem to be destroyed. Fortunately this direction was disregarded by his literary executors.

The second book of the Aeneid, the subject of this edition, is one of the most interesting for modern readers, for it describes the final siege and capture of Troy, and fully illustrates Vergil's great poetical genius, his technical mastery of the hexameter, his brilliant similes, his sympathy with humanity and nature, and his deep appreciation of the spiritual side of life. The second book also reveals the weakness of the hero of the epic, Aeneas, who, throughout the poem remains an uninspiring figure that fails to win from the reader the admiration and respect he receives from his followers. Perhaps Vergil's temperament was unable to appreciate and so bring to life men of action.

The story of the epic is as follows.

BOOK I. Aeneas and his companions are driven by a storm aroused by Juno, the implacable enemy of the Trojan race, towards the North African coast, where, thanks to the intervention of Neptune, most of the ships find shelter, their crews landing safely and making their way to Carthage. In this city, which has just been founded by Dido, a young widow from Tyre, they are hospitably received by the queen, who, at a banquet, invites Aeneas to relate the story of his wanderings.

BOOK II. The Trojan hero begins his narrative with the story of the final siege, capture and sack of Troy. We hear of the treacherous Sinon, the trick of the wooden horse, the cruel death of Laocoon and his sons, the murder of Priam and the escape of Aeneas from the burning city with his aged father Anchises, his young son Iulus (or Ascanius) and the household gods. In the confusion, his wife Creusa is lost, but later, Aeneas meets her ghost and is told that he is destined to found a new kingdom in Italy.

BOOK III. The narrative continues with the escape of Aeneas and his Trojan comrades from the mainland, and their voyage to various places in search of the ' promised land ', to Thrace, Delos, Crete, and finally to the west, by way of the Strophades Islands, and the coast of Epirus (Albania) where Aeneas is advised by Helenus to sail round

Sicily, to make for the west coast of Italy and there to consult the prophetess Sibyl at Cumae and appease Juno. Aeneas does as Helenus suggests, and thus, after seven years' wandering over the Eastern Mediterranean, he arrives at the western end of Sicily, where he spends the winter. Anchises, his father, dies. At this point Aeneas ends his narrative.

BOOK IV. Meanwhile Dido, who has been greatly attracted to Aeneas from the first owing to the influence of Venus, Aeneas' mother, now falls more and more deeply in love with the Trojan leader. Shortly after his arrival at Carthage, again owing to the intrigues of Venus, they are united in love. Jupiter, however, now intervenes and warns Aeneas by Mercury that he must leave Africa at once and fulfil his destined task of founding a new realm in Italy. Realising the strength of Dido's passion for him, he tries to depart secretly, but is discovered. Yet he remains unmoved by the queen's entreaties, which quickly turn to scorn. As he sails away, Dido commits suicide.

BOOK V. Aeneas returns to western Sicily and celebrates there the anniversary of his father's death with funeral games.[1] During the latter, Juno per-

[1] The elaborate description of these, which occupies most of the fifth book, is no doubt due to the influence of Homer, who devoted the twenty-third book of the Iliad to the funeral games of Patroclus.

suades the Trojan women, weary as they are of their wanderings, to set fire to the ships, but a sudden rainstorm subdues the flames and only four are destroyed.

The Trojans sail away from Sicily, and Palinurus, the helmsman, is overcome by sleep and, falling overboard, is drowned.

Book VI. In this, to many readers the finest book of the poem, Aeneas visits the Sibyl of Cumae and receives from her detailed instructions as to his proposed visit to the underworld. Armed with the ' golden bough ' which alone could gain him access to the world below, he traverses the various quarters of that kingdom, and beholds the spirit of his father, who parades for his son the souls of all great Romans that are awaiting incarnation.[1] In this way Vergil is able to give his readers a kind of national cavalcade of all the great figures in Roman history from the earliest times until his own day. Thus the procession is closed with the greatest figure of them all, the emperor Augustus.

The sixth book contains the famous lines (851–3) which summarise the Roman's pride in his greatness as an imperial power.

> Tu regere imperio populos, Romane, memento ;
> Hae tibi erunt artes ; pacisque imponere morem,
> Parcere subiectis, et debellare superbos.

[1] An adaptation of the visit of Odysseus to the underworld in the XIth book of Homer's Odyssey.

'Thou, O Roman, remember to rule the nations 'neath thy
   sway.
These shall be thine arts, to impose the laws of peace,
To spare the conquered and to chasten the proud in war.'

BOOK VII. Aeneas at last enters Italy, the
promised land, by the mouth of the river Tiber,
nature's boundary between the districts of Latium,
lying south of the river, and Etruria to the north.
He is welcomed by Latinus, king of Latium, who
sees in Aeneas the bridegroom for his daughter
Lavinia, for whom he has been advised by an
oracle to find a foreign husband.

Turnus, however, chieftain of the neighbouring
Rutuli, and goodliest of Lavinia's suitors, is enraged
at Latinus' proposal, and, supported by Amata,
Latinus' queen, arouses the Latins against the
Trojans. The book closes with a magnificent catalogue of the Italian forces (another epic convention,
originati g in Homer's catalogue of the Greek ships
in the Iliad, Book II).

BOOK VIII. The god of the Tiber sends Aeneas
to seek aid from the Greek Evander who has settled
on the Palatine Hill in what is destined to be the
future Rome. Evander promises help and conducts
Aeneas through the city, explaining the origin of
various Roman sites and names. Venus persuades
Vulcan, her husband, to make Aeneas a suit of

armour, on the shield of which are described various events in the future history of Rome down to the battle of Actium.[1]

Book IX. While Aeneas is absent, Turnus just fails to storm the Trojan camp by the Tiber, but sets their ships on fire. Nisus and Euryalus, two Trojans, endeavour to slip through the enemy lines in order to inform Aeneas of the critical state of affairs. They inflict some casualties, but eventually are discovered and killed. The next day when Turnus renews his assault, he succeeds in getting within the camp, but he is cut off, effecting an escape only by plunging into the Tiber.

Book X. A council of the gods is held in Olympus and Jupiter decides to leave the issue of the war to fate. Aeneas now wins the support of an Etruscan army which has revolted against the cruelties of their king Mezentius, and joined by reinforcements from Evander under the leadership of Pallas,[2] he returns to aid the hard-pressed Trojans. In the furious fighting, Mezentius and his son Lausus are slain and Turnus kills Pallas.

Book XI. A truce is arranged for the burial of the dead. On the arrival of an embassy from the

---

[1] Another epic convention—an imitation of Homer's description of Achilles' shield in the XVIIIth book of the Iliad.

[2] Evander's son.

Latins, Aeneas offers to settle the issue by a single combat between himself and Turnus. The Latins hold a council of war and determine to continue the struggle, but they are defeated a second time by the Trojans and their allies, in spite of many deeds of valour, especially on the part of Camilla, an Amazonian heroine who is killed in the fighting.

BOOK XII. Another truce is arranged, and Turnus is ready to accept Aeneas' challenge despite the opposition of the queen Amata and his sister Iuturna. The latter provokes the Latins to violate the truce. In the fighting Aeneas is wounded, but later miraculously healed by his goddess mother Venus. He returns to the fight, routs the Latins and Rutulians and eventually meets Turnus in single combat. The Rutulian chieftain is wounded. Aeneas is minded to spare him till he notices that he is wearing the belt of the dead Pallas. Whereupon he slays him.

THE METRE OF THE POEM

Most English verse consists of lines in which stressed syllables alternate with unstressed, as for example in the line :

'The ploughman homeward plods his weary way
And leaves the world to darkness and to me.'

Such verse is called *accentual*.

The principle of Greek and Latin verse is different. It is based on the rhythmical arrangement of long and short syllables, the long syllables taking twice as long to pronounce as the short. This system may be compared with music, long syllables corresponding to *crotchets* and short to *quavers*, one *crotchet* being equal to two *quavers*. This type of verse is called *quantitative*.

Just as, to appreciate the rhythm of English verse, you are taught to *scan*, i.e. divide the lines into *feet* and mark the stress in each foot, so you must learn to scan Latin verse by a similar division into feet and by marking the syllables long (–) or short (◡). Not only is it necessary to do this in order to understand the construction of the verse and the musical qualities of the poetry, but the ability to do it is a great help in translation, by making it possible to distinguish words alike in spelling but different in *quantity*, for example pŏpŭlŭs, *people*, from pōpŭlŭs, *poplar tree*.

The verses of the Aeneid are called heroic hexameters. In this verse two kinds of feet, or bars, are found. One is the *dactyl*, a long syllable followed by two short syllables, the other, the *spondee*, two long syllables. Each line, or hexameter, contains six feet, the first four of which may be either dactyls or spondees, the fifth being almost always a dactyl,

and the sixth a spondee. In place of this sixth foot
spondee a trochee (–◡) is allowable.

Thus the scheme of the hexameter is as follows :

	1	2	3	4	5	6
	– ◡ ◡	– ◡ ◡	– ◡ ◡	– ◡ ◡	– ◡ ◡	– –
or	– –	– –	– –	– –		– ◡

In the scansion of these lines, no account is taken
of syllables at the close of a word *ending* in a vowel
or an *m*, if they are followed immediately by a word
commencing with a vowel or an *h*. Such a final
syllable is said to be *elided*, ' struck out ', though it
was more probably slurred in pronunciation. Thus
in l. 1, which begins *conticuere omnes*, the final *e* of
conticuere is ignored in scanning.

A long syllable is one that contains a vowel long
by nature, or a diphthong ; or a vowel, naturally
short, that is long *by position*, i.e., is followed by two
consonants.

A short syllable is one that contains a vowel short
by nature and ends either with no consonant, or with
only one.

The two consonants which have been mentioned
as having the effect of lengthening a syllable need
not both occur in the one word. Thus in line 3, the
final syllable of *infandum* is long, though the *u* is
naturally short, because that *u* is followed by *m* and
the *r* of *regina*.

PROSODY.

The following information about the quantity of Latin syllables will be found useful.

A. Relating to all syllables.

All diphthongs are long, except before another vowel.

B. Relating to final syllables.

1. Final *a* is usually short.

Except

    (*a*) in the abl. sg. of 1st decl. nouns, e.g. *mensā* ;

    (*b*) in the 2nd sg. imperative active of 1st conjugation verbs, e.g. *amā* ;

    (*c*) in indeclinable words like *intereā, frustrā.*

2. Final *e* is usually short.

Except

    (*a*) in the abl. sg. of 5th decl. nouns, e.g. *aciē* ;

    (*b*) in the 2nd sg. imperative active of 2nd conjugation verbs, e.g. *monē* ;

    (*c*) in adverbs formed from adjectives in *-us, -a, -um*, e.g. *pulchrē*. Note however *benĕ, malĕ.*

3. Final *i* is usually long.

Except in *mihi, tibi, sibi, ubi, ibi*, in which it may be long or short, and in *quasi, nisi.*

4. Final *o* is usually long.

Except in *modo, duo, ego.*

C. Final syllables of words of more than one syllable, ending in any single consonant other than *s*, are short.

Except

(*a*) *dispăr* ;

(*b*) in the perfects *iĭt* and *petiĭt*.

D. 1. Final *as*, *os*, *es*, are long.

Except

(*a*) *compŏs*, *penĕs* ;

(*b*) in nominatives singular in *es* of 3rd declension nouns (consonant stems) having genitive sg. in *-ĕtis*, *-ĭtis*, *-idis* : e.g. *segĕs*, *milĕs*, *obsĕs*. (But note *pariēs*, *abiēs*, *Cerēs*.)

(*c*) in compounds of *es* (from *sum*), e.g. *abĕs*, *prodĕs*.

2. Final *us* and *is* are short.

Except *ūs*

(*a*) in gen. sg., nom., voc. and acc. pl. of 4th declension nouns, e.g. *gradūs*, *genūs*.

(*b*) in the nom. sg. of consonant stem 3rd declension nouns having gen. sg. with a long penultimate syllable, e.g. *tellūs* (*-ūris*), *palūs* (*-ūdis*), *virtūs* (*-ūtis*).

And except *īs*

(*c*) in dat. and abl. pl., e.g. *mensīs*, *dominīs*, *vinīs*.

(*d*) in nom. and acc. pl. of 3rd declension -*i*
stems, e.g. *omnīs, navīs.*

(*e*) in the 2nd pers. sg. of 4th conjugation
verbs, e.g. *audīs* ; and in *sīs,* and compounds of *sīs,* as *possīs* ; and in *velīs,
nolīs, malīs,* and *īs* (from *eo*).

E. Quantity of syllables determined by position in
the same word.

1. A syllable ending with a vowel or diphthong,
immediately followed by a syllable beginning with a
vowel, or with *h* and a vowel, is short : e.g. *vĭa,
prăeustus, trăhit.*

Except

(*a*) in the case of genitives in -*ius,* e.g. *alīus,
solīus, utrīus.* (But not *illĭus.*)

(*b*) *e* preceding *i* in 5th declension, e.g. *diĕi,* and
in *ĕi* (from *is*).

(*c*) the syllable *fĭ* in *fĭo.* (But note *fieri,
fierem,* the *i* being short before *er.*)

2. A syllable containing a vowel immediately
followed by two consonants, or by *x* or *z,* which are
really double consonants (*cs* and *ds*) is long ; e.g.
regent, auspex.

Except

(*a*) if the two consonants are a combination of
one of the following, *b, c, d, f, g, p, t,* with
(following) *l* or *r.*

If a short vowel precedes such a combination the syllable is not necessarily long.

Finally it must be remembered that these rules apply to Latin words only, and not to several Greek proper names which will be met with in this book.

Let us now see if, with the information given above, we can scan one of the hexameters of this poem.

Looking at the tenth line,

>   *sed si tantus amor casus cognoscere nostros*

(i) see first whether any syllable requires to be *elided*, i.e. not taken into account.   (There is none; although elision is frequent in Vergil.)

(ii) mark long (-) all syllables whose long quantity can be determined by the rules given above.

>   *sed, tan, mor, sus, cog, nos, nos*

are all long syllables (by Rule E 2), giving us now

>   *sēd si tāntus amōr casus cōgnoscere nōstros*

(iii) mark short all syllables whose short quantity can be determined by rule.

The final *tus* of *tantus*, and the final *re* of *cognoscere* are short by Rule D 2 and B 2, giving us

>   *sēd si tāntŭs amōr casūs cōgnoscerĕ nōstros.*

Now work backwards from the end of the line,

because the pattern of the last two feet ($-\;\smallsmile\;\smallsmile\;|\;-\;-$ or $-\;\smallsmile$) is constant. This gives us, for these feet,

$$\overset{5}{|\;\bar{no}\bar{s}c\breve{e}r\breve{e}}\;\;\overset{6}{|\;\bar{no}\bar{s}tr\bar{o}s}$$

(*rōs* is long by Rule D 1).

Working backwards again, the fourth foot is obviously a spondee :

$$\overset{4}{\cdot}$$
$$|\;\bar{sus}\;\bar{cog}\;|$$

and the 3rd, a spondee,

$$\overset{3}{|\;\bar{mor}\;\bar{ca}\;|}$$

This leaves us with five syllables to be got into the first two feet, which must thus consist of one spondee and one dactyl :

$$\overset{\text{I}}{\bar{Sed}\;\bar{si}}\;|\;\overset{2}{\bar{tan}t\breve{u}s\;\breve{a}}\;|.$$

And the whole line, divided into feet and with the quantities marked, is

$$\overset{\text{I}}{\bar{sed}\;\bar{si}}\;|\;\overset{2}{\bar{tan}t\breve{u}s\;\breve{a}}\;|\;\overset{3}{\bar{mor}\;\bar{ca}}\;|\;\overset{4}{\bar{sus}\;\bar{cog}}\;|\;\overset{5}{\bar{no}\bar{s}c\breve{e}r\breve{e}}\;|\;\overset{6}{\bar{no}\bar{s}tr\bar{o}s}$$

One thing remains to be done before our scansion is complete. It is a rule that usually in the 3rd foot, more rarely in the 4th, one word must end and another begin. This is called the *caesura* or ' cutting '. If this break occurs after the first syllable of the foot, the caesura is said to be *strong* ; if after the second, *weak*. In this line we obviously have a strong caesura in the 3rd foot. The caesura is regularly marked in scansion by a pair of vertical lines.

Thus the scansion of our line, as completed, is

$$s\bar{e}d \; \bar{s}i \mid t\bar{a}nt\breve{u}s \; \breve{a} \mid m\bar{o}r \mid\mid c\bar{a} \mid s\bar{u}s \; c\bar{o}g \mid n\bar{o}sc\breve{e}r\breve{e} \mid n\bar{o}str\bar{o}s$$

You will find that, with careful attention to the pronunciation of Latin words, you will gradually learn to scan by ear, without the necessity of applying for help to the rules of prosody. You should try to develop this power as early as possible.

Note that the scheme of the hexameter makes it elastic and gives it a variable length, as long as 17 or as short as 13 syllables. This makes possible such lines as

$$qu\bar{a}dr\breve{u}p\breve{e} \mid d\bar{a}nt\breve{e} \; p\breve{u} \mid tr\bar{e}m \; s\breve{o}n\breve{i} \mid t\bar{u} \; qu\breve{a}tit \mid \bar{u}ng\breve{u}l\breve{a} \mid$$
$$c\bar{a}mp\breve{u}m$$

(where the poet, describing the galloping of horses, imitates the sound of them),
and as

$$ill(i) \; \bar{i}n \mid t\bar{e}r \; s\bar{e} \mid s\bar{e} \; m\bar{a}g \mid n\bar{a} \; v\bar{i} \mid br\bar{a}cch\breve{i}\breve{a} \mid t\bar{o}ll\bar{u}nt$$

(where again sound is matched to sense, for the line describes the alternate blows upon an anvil delivered by two smiths).

VERGIL
AENEID II

Aeneas, urged by Dido to tell her of the fall of Troy,
begins with the building of the Wooden Horse

Conticuere omnes intentique ora tenebant.
Inde toro pater Aeneas sic orsus ab alto :
  Infandum, regina, iubes renovare dolorem,
Troianas ut opes et lamentabile regnum
eruerint Danai, quaeque ipse miserrima vidi,   5
et quorum pars magna fui.   Quis talia fando
Myrmidonum Dolopumve aut duri miles Ulixi
temperet a lacrimis?   Et iam nox umida caelo
praecipitat suadentque cadentia sidera somnos.
Sed si tantus amor casus cognoscere nostros,   10
et breviter Troiae supremum audire laborem,
quamquam animus meminisse horret luctuque
       refugit,
incipiam.
            Fracti bello fatisque repulsi
ductores Danaum, tot iam labentibus annis,
instar montis equum divina Palladis arte   15
aedificant, sectaque intexunt abiete costas ;
votum pro reditu simulant ; ea fama vagatur.

Huc delecta virum sortiti corpora furtim
includunt caeco lateri, penitusque cavernas
ingentis uterumque armato milite complent. 20

The Trojans discuss what to do with the Horse

Est in conspectu Tenedos, notissima fama
insula, dives opum, Priami dum regna manebant,
nunc tantum sinus, et statio male fida carinis :
huc se provecti deserto in litore condunt.
Nos abiisse rati et vento petiisse Mycenas. 25
Ergo omnis longo solvit se Teucria luctu.
Panduntur portae ; iuvat ire et Dorica castra
desertosque videre locos litusque relictum.
Hic Dolopum manus, hic saevus tendebat Achilles ;
classibus hic locus, hic acie certare solebant. 30
Pars stupet innuptae donum exitiale Minervae,
et molem mirantur equi ; primusque Thymoetes
duci intra muros hortatur et arce locari,
sive dolo seu iam Troiae sic fata ferebant.
At Capys, et quorum melior sententia menti, 35
aut pelago Danaum insidias suspectaque dona
praecipitare iubent, subiectisve urere flammis :
aut terebrare cavas uteri et temptare latebras.
Scinditur incertum studia in contraria vulgus.

The priest Laocoon suspects a stratagem and warns
the Trojans

Primus ibi ante omnis, magna comitante caterva,
Laocoon ardens summa decurrit ab arce,   41
et procul : 'o miseri, quae tanta insania, cives?
Creditis avectos hostis? aut ulla putatis
dona carere dolis Danaum? sic notus Ulixes?
Aut hoc inclusi ligno occultantur Achivi,   45
aut haec in nostros fabricata est machina muros,
inspectura domos venturaque desuper urbi,
aut aliquis latet error : equo ne credite, Teucri.
Quidquid id est, timeo Danaos et dona ferentis.'
Sic fatus validis ingentem viribus hastam   50
in latus inque feri curvam compagibus alvum
contorsit. Stetit illa tremens, uteroque recusso
insonuere cavae gemitumque dedere cavernae.
Et, si fata deum, si mens non laeva fuisset,
impulerat ferro Argolicas foedare latebras,   55
Troiaque nunc staret, Priamique arx alta, maneres.

A prisoner is brought in by some Trojan shepherds

Ecce, manus iuvenem interea post terga revinctum
pastores magno ad regem clamore trahebant
Dardanidae, qui se ignotum venientibus ultro,
hoc ipsum ut strueret Troiamque aperiret Achivis, 60
obtulerat, fidens animi atque in utrumque paratus,
seu versare dolos, seu certae occumbere morti.

Undique visendi studio Troiana iuventus
circumfusa ruit, certantque inludere capto.
Accipe nunc Danaum insidias, et crimine ab uno   65
disce omnis.

Namque ut conspectu in medio turbatus, inermis,
cɔnstitit, atque oculis Phrygia agmina circumspexit :
' Heu, quae nunc tellus,' inquit, ' quae me aequora
    possunt
accipere?   Aut quid iam misero mihi denique restat,
cui neque apud Danaos usquam locus, et super ipsi 71
Dardanidae infensi poenas cum sanguine poscunt? '
Quo gemitu conversi animi, compressus et omnis
impetus.   Hortamur fari, quo sanguine cretus,
quidve ferat ; memoret, quae sit fiducia capto.   75
Ille haec, deposita tandem formidine, fatur :

The prisoner, one Sinon, tells a story that rouses the
curiosity of the Trojans

' Cuncta equidem tibi, rex, fuerit quodcumque,
    fatebor
vera,' inquit : ' neque me Argolica de gente negabo :
hoc primum ; nec, si miserum fortuna Sinonem
finxit, vanum etiam mendacemque, improba, finget.
Fando aliquod si forte tuas pervenit ad auris   81
Belidae nomen Palamedis et incluta fama
gloria, quem falsa sub proditione Pelasgi
insontem infando indicio, quia bella vetabat,

demisere neci, nunc cassum lumine lugent ;   85
illi me comitem et consanguinitate propinquum
pauper in arma pater primis huc misit ab annis.
Dum stabat regno incolumis, regumque vigebat
conciliis, et nos aliquod nomenque decusque
gessimus.   Invidia postquam pellacis Ulixi   90
(haud ignota loquor) superis concessit ab oris,
adflictus vitam in tenebris luctuque trahebam,
et casum insontis mecum indignabar amici.
Nec tacui demens ; et me, fors si qua tulisset,
si patrios unquam remeassem victor ad Argos,   95
promisi ultorem, et verbis odia aspera movi.
Hinc mihi prima mali labes, hinc semper Ulixes
criminibus terrere novis, hinc spargere voces
in vulgum ambiguas, et quaerere conscius arma.
Nec requievit enim, donec Calchante ministro— 100
sed quid ego haec autem nequiquam ingrata revolvo?
Quidve moror? Si omnis uno ordine habetis Achivos,
idque audire sat est, iamdudum sumite poenas :
hoc Ithacus velit et magno mercentur Atridae.'
Tum vero ardemus scitari et quaerere causas,   105
ignari scelerum tantorum artisque Pelasgae.
Prosequitur pavitans, et ficto pectore fatur :

The false Sinon pretends to be a deserter from the Greeks

' Saepe fugam Danai Troia cupiere relicta
moliri et longo fessi discedere bello ;

fecissent utinam!   Saepe illos aspera ponti   110
interclusit hiems, et terruit Auster euntis.
Praecipue, cum iam hic trabibus contextus acernis
staret equus, toto sonuerunt aethere nimbi.
Suspensi Eurypylum scitantem oracula Phoebi 114
mittimus ; isque adytis haec tristia dicta reportat :
' Sanguine placastis ventos et virgine caesa,
cum primum Iliacas, Danai, venistis ad oras :
sanguine quaerendi reditus, animaque litandum
Argolica.'   Vulgi quae vox ut venit ad auris,
obstupuere animi, gelidusque per ima cucurrit   120
ossa tremor, cui fata parent, quem poscat Apollo.
Hic Ithacus vatem magno Calchanta tumultu
protrahit in medios ; quae sint ea numina divum,
flagitat.   Et mihi iam multi crudele canebant
artificis scelus, et taciti ventura videbant.   125
Bis quinos silet ille dies, tectusque recusat
prodere voce sua quemquam aut opponere morti.
Vix tandem, magnis Ithaci clamoribus actus,
composito rumpit vocem et me destinat arae.
Adsensere omnes et, quae sibi quisque timebat, 130
unius in miseri exitium conversa tulere.
Iamque dies infanda aderat ; mihi sacra parari,
et salsae fruges, et circum tempora vittae.
Eripui, fateor, leto me, et vincula rupi ;
limosoque lacu per noctem obscurus in ulva   135
delitui, dum vela darent, si forte dedissent.

Nec mihi iam patriam antiquam spes ulla videndi,
nec dulcis natos exoptatumque parentem ;
quos illi fors et poenas ob nostra reposcent
effugia, et culpam hanc miserorum morte piabunt. 140
Quod te per superos et conscia numina veri,
per, si qua est, quae restet adhuc mortalibus usquam
intemerata fides, oro, miserere laborum
tantorum, miserere animi non digna ferentis.'

*Sinon's lying tale deceives the Trojans. Asked by Priam to
explain the purpose of the Wooden Horse he is fertile in
fresh inventions*

His lacrimis vitam damus, et miserescimus ultro.
Ipse viro primus manicas atque arta levari   146
vincla iubet Priamus, dictisque ita fatur amicis :
' Quisquis es, amissos hinc iam obliviscere Graios :
noster eris ; mihique haec edissere vera roganti :
quo molem hanc immanis equi statuere? Quis
    auctor?   150
Quidve petunt? Quae religio aut quae machina
    belli? '
Dixerat. Ille, dolis instructus et arte Pelasga,
sustulit exutas vinclis ad sidera palmas :
' Vos aeterni ignes, et non violabile vestrum
testor numen,' ait, ' vos arae ensesque nefandi, 155
quos fugi, vittaeque deum, quas hostia gessi :
fas mihi Graiorum sacrata resolvere iura,
fas odisse viros, atque omnia ferre sub auras,

si qua tegunt ; teneor patriae nec legibus ullis.
Tu modo promissis maneas, servataque serves   160
Troia fidem, si vera feram, si magna rependam.
  'Omnis spes Danaum et coepti fiducia belli
Palladis auxiliis semper stetit.   Impius ex quo
Tydides sed enim scelerumque inventor Ulixes,
fatale adgressi sacrato avellere templo   165
Palladium, caesis summae custodibus arcis,
corripuere sacram effigiem, manibusque cruentis
virgineas ausi divae contingere vittas ;
ex illo fluere ac retro sublapsa referri
spes Danaum, fractae vires, aversa deae mens.   170
Nec dubiis ea signa dedit Tritonia monstris.
Vix positum castris simulacrum, arsere coruscae
luminibus flammae arrectis, salsusque per artus
sudor iit, terque ipsa solo (mirabile dictu),   174
emicuit, parmamque ferens hastamque trementem.
Extemplo temptanda fuga canit aequora Calchas,
nec posse Argolicis exscindi Pergama telis,
omina ni repetant Argis, numenque reducant,
quod pelago et curvis secum avexere carinis.
Et nunc, quod patrias vento petiere Mycenas,   180
arma deosque parant comites, pelagoque remenso
improvisi aderunt.   Ita digerit omina Calchas.
Hanc pro Palladio moniti, pro numine laeso
effigiem statuere, nefas quae triste piaret.
Hanc tamen immensam Calchas attollere molem 185

roboribus textis caeloque educere iussit,
ne recipi portis aut duci in moenia possit,
neu populum antiqua sub religione tueri.
Nam si vestra manus violasset dona Minervae,   189
tum magnum exitium (quod di prius omen in
   ipsum
convertant!) Priami imperio Phrygibusque futurum ;
sin manibus vestris vestram ascendisset in urbem,
ultro Asiam magno Pelopea ad moenia bello
venturam, et nostros ea fata manere nepotes.'

Laocoon is destroyed by two sea-monsters sent by Pallas

Talibus insidiis periurique arte Sinonis   195
credita res, captique dolis lacrimisque coactis,
quos neque Tydides, nec Larissaeus Achilles,
non anni domuere decem, non mille carinae.
   Hic aliud maius miseris multoque tremendum
obicitur magis, atque improvida pectora turbat.   200
Laocoon, ductus Neptuni sorte sacerdos,
sollemnis taurum ingentem mactabat ad aras.
Ecce autem gemini a Tenedo tranquilla per alta
(horresco referens) immensis orbibus angues
incumbunt pelago, pariterque ad litora tendunt ; 205
pectora quorum inter fluctus arrecta iubaeque
sanguineae superant undas ; pars cetera pontum
pone legit, sinuatque immensa volumine terga.

Fit sonitus spumante salo : iamque arva tenebant,
ardentisque oculos suffecti sanguine et igni   210
sibila lambebant linguis vibrantibus ora.
Diffugimus visu exsangues.   Illi agmine certo
Laocoonta petunt.   Et primum parva duorum
corpora natorum serpens amplexus uterque
implicat, et miseros morsu depascitur artus ;   215
post ipsum, auxilio subeuntem ac tela ferentem,
corripiunt, spirisque ligant ingentibus ; et iam
bis medium amplexi, bis collo squamea circum
terga dati, superant capite et cervicibus altis.
Ille simul manibus tendit divellere nodos,   220
perfusus sanie vittas atroque veneno ;
clamores simul horrendos ad sidera tollit :
qualis mugitus, fugit cum saucius aram
taurus et incertam excussit cervice securim.
At gemini lapsu delubra ad summa dracones   225
effugiunt, saevaeque petunt Tritonidis arcem,
sub pedibusque deae, clipeique sub orbe teguntur.

The fate of Laocoon, who had violated the Horse, decides the
Trojans to breach their walls and bring it into the city

Tum vero tremefacta novus per pectora cunctis
insinuat pavor ; et scelus expendisse merentem
Laocoonta ferunt, sacrum qui cuspide robur   230
laeserit, et tergo sceleratam intorserit hastam.
Ducendum ad sedes simulacrum, orandaque divae
numina conclamant.
Dividimus muros et moenia pandimus urbis.
Accingunt omnes operi, pedibusque rotarum   235
subiciunt lapsus, et stuppea vincula collo
intendunt.   Scandit fatalis machina muros,
feta armis.   Pueri circum innuptaeque puellae
sacra canunt funemque manu contingere gaudent.
Illa subit, mediaeque minans inlabitur urbi.   240
O patria, o divum domus Ilium, et incluta bello
moenia Dardanidum! Quater ipso in limine portae
substitit, atque utero sonitum quater arma dedere.
Instamus tamen immemores caecique furore,
et monstrum infelix sacrata sistimus arce.   245
Tunc etiam fatis aperit Cassandra futuris
ora, dei iussu non unquam credita Teucris.
Nos delubra deum miseri, quibus ultimus esset
ille dies, festa velamus fronde per urbem.
    Vertitur interea caelum, et ruit Oceano nox,   250
involvens umbra magna terramque polumque

Myrmidonumque dolos ; fusi per moenia Teucri
conticuere ; sopor fessos complectitur artus.
Et iam Argiva phalanx instructis navibus ibat
a Tenedo, tacitae per amica silentia lunae   255
litora nota petens, flammas cum regia puppis
extulerat, fatisque deum defensus iniquis,
inclusos utero Danaos et pinea furtim
laxat claustra Sinon.   Illos patefactus ad auras
reddit equus, laetique cavo se robore promunt   260
Thessandrus Sthenelusque duces et dirus Ulixes,
demissum lapsi per funem, Acamasque, Thoasque,
Pelidesque Neoptolemus, primusque Machaon,

' Illos patefactus ad auras
reddit equus, laetique cavo se robore promunt.'

Trojan Horse from C7th Greek relief vase, Mykonos.

et Menelaus, et ipse doli fabricator Epeos.

Invadunt urbem somno vinoque sepultam ;   265

caeduntur vigiles, portisque patentibus omnis

accipiunt socios, atque agmina conscia iungunt.

Hector's ghost, appearing to Aeneas, warns him of
Troy's approaching doom

Tempus erat, quo prima quies mortalibus aegris

incipit, et dono divum gratissima serpit.

In somnis, ecce, ante oculos maestissimus Hector 270

visus adesse mihi, largosque effundere fletus,

raptatus bigis, ut quondam, aterque cruento

pulvere, perque pedes traiectus lora tumentis.

Ei mihi, qualis erat!   Quantum mutatus ab illo

Hectore, qui redit exuvias indutus Achilli,   275

vel Danaum Phrygios iaculatus puppibus ignis!

squalentem barbam, et concretos sanguine crinis,

vulneraque illa gerens, quae circum plurima muros

accepit patrios.   Ultro flens ipse videbar

compellare virum, et maestas expromere voces : 280

' O lux Dardaniae, spes o fidissima Teucrum,

quae tantae tenuere morae?   Quibus Hector ab oris

exspectate venis?   Ut te post multa tuorum

funera, post varios hominumque urbisque labores

defessi aspicimus!   Quae causa indigna serenos   285

foedavit vultus?   Aut cur haec vulnera cerno? '

Ille nihil ; nec me quaerentem vana moratur :

HECTOR'S BODY DRAGGED BEHIND THE CHARIOT OF ACHILLES.

The winged figure is the ghost of Hector's victim Patroclus ; the charioteer is Automedon, and Achilles, helmeted, is seen behind the horses. (From a Greek vase of about 500 B.C.)

sed graviter gemitus imo de pectore ducens,
' Heu! fuge, nate dea, teque his,' ait, ' eripe flammis.
Hostis habet muros ; ruit alto a culmine Troia. 290
Sat patriae Priamoque datum. Si Pergama dextra
defendi possent, etiam hac defensa fuissent.
Sacra suosque tibi commendat Troia Penatis ;
hos cape fatorum comites ; his moenia quaere,
magna pererrato statues quae denique ponto.' 295
Sic ait, et manibus vittas Vestamque potentem
aeternumque adytis effert penetralibus ignem.

*Aeneas wakes from his vision, to see and hear the
truth of Hector's warning*

Diverso interea miscentur moenia luctu ;
et magis atque magis, quamquam secreta parentis
Anchisae domus arboribusque obtecta recessit, 300
clarescunt sonitus, armorumque ingruit horror.
Excutior somno, et summi fastigia tecti
ascensu supero, atque arrectis auribus adsto :
in segetem veluti cum flamma furentibus Austris
incidit, aut rapidus montano flumine torrens 305
sternit agros, sternit sata laeta boumque labores,
praecipitesque trahit silvas ; stupet inscius alto
accipiens sonitum saxi de vertice pastor.
Tum vero manifesta fides, Danaumque patescunt
insidiae. Iam Deïphobi dedit ampla ruinam, 310
Volcano superante, domus ; iam proximus ardet

Ucalegon ; Sigea igni freta lata relucent :
exoritur clamorque virum clangorque tubarum.
Arma amens capio ; nec sat rationis in armis,
sed glomerare manum bello et concurrere in arcem
cum sociis ardent animi.   Furor iraque mentem 316
praecipitant, pulchrumque mori succurrit in armis.

Panthus, priest of Apollo, tells Aeneas that resistance
is hopeless

Start —▶
②

Ecce autem telis Panthus elapsus Achivum,
Panthus Othryades, arcis Phoebique sacerdos,
sacra manu victosque deos parvumque nepotem 320
ipse trahit, cursuque amens ad limina tendit.
' Quo res summa loco, Panthu?   Quam prendimus
    arcem? '
Vix ea fatus eram, gemitu cum talia reddit :
' Venit summa dies et ineluctabile tempus
Dardaniae.   Fuimus Troes, fuit Ilium et ingens 325
gloria Teucrorum.   Ferus omnia Iuppiter Argos
transtulit : incensa Danai dominantur in urbe.
Arduus armatos mediis in moenibus adstans
fundit equus, victorque Sinon incendia miscet

End —▶
②

insultans.   Portis alii bipatentibus adsunt,   330
milia quot magnis umquam venere Mycenis ;
obsedere alii telis angusta viarum
oppositis ; stat ferri acies mucrone corusco
stricta, parata neci ; vix primi proelia temptant
portarum vigiles, et caeco Marte resistunt.'   335

*Aeneas, however, gathers a band of warriors to make
what resistance is possible*

Talibus Othryadae dictis et numine divum
in flammas et in arma feror, quo tristis Erinys,
quo fremitus vocat et sublatus ad aethera clamor.
Addunt se socios Ripheus et maximus armis   339
Epytus, oblati per lunam, Hypanisque Dymasque,
et lateri adglomerant nostro, iuvenisque Coroebus
Mygdonides.   Illis ad Troiam forte diebus
venerat, insano Cassandrae incensus amore,
et gener auxilium Priamo Phrygibusque ferebat—
infelix, qui non sponsae praecepta furentis   345
audierit.
Quos ubi confertos audere in proelia vidi,
incipio super his : ' Iuvenes, fortissima frustra
pectora, si vobis audentem extrema cupido
certa sequi, quae sit rebus fortuna videtis.   350
Excessere omnes, adytis arisque relictis,
di, quibus imperium hoc steterat ; succurritis urbi
incensae ; moriamur, et in media arma ruamus.
Una salus victis—nullam sperare salutem.'
Sic animis iuvenum furor additus. Inde, lupi ceu 355
raptores atra in nebula, quos improba ventris
exegit caecos rabies, catulique relicti
faucibus exspectant siccis, per tela, per hostis
vadimus haud dubiam in mortem, mediaeque tene-
      mus

urbis iter : nox atra cava circumvolat umbra.   360
Quis cladem illius noctis, quis funera fando
explicet, aut possit lacrimis aequare labores?
Urbs antiqua ruit, multos dominata per annos :
plurima perque vias sternuntur inertia passim
corpora, perque domos et religiosa deorum   365
limina. Nec soli poenas dant sanguine Teucri :
quondam etiam victis redit in praecordia virtus,
victoresque cadunt Danai. Crudelis ubique
luctus, ubique pavor, et plurima mortis imago.

*Taking the arms and accoutrements of some Greeks whom they
   overwhelm, Aeneas and his comrades, thus disguised,
   gain some successes*

Primus se, Danaum magna comitante caterva, 370
Androgeos offert nobis, socia agmina credens
inscius, atque ultro verbis compellat amicis :
' Festinate, viri : nam quae tam sera moratur
segnities? Alii rapiunt incensa feruntque   374
Pergama : vos celsis nunc primum a navibus itis '?
Dixit ; et extemplo—neque enim responsa dabantur
fida satis—sensit medios delapsus in hostis.
Obstupuit, retroque pedem cum voce repressit.
Improvisum aspris veluti qui sentibus anguem
pressit humi nitens, trepidusque repente refugit 380
attollentem iras, et caerula colla tumentem :
haud secus Androgeos visu tremefactus abibat.

Inruimus densis et circumfundimur armis,
ignarosque loci passim et formidine captos
sternimus.   Adspirat primo fortuna labori.   385
Atque hic successu exsultans animisque Coroebus,
' O socii, qua prima,' inquit, ' fortuna salutis
monstrat iter, quaque ostendit se dextra, sequamur :
mutemus clipeos, Danaumque insignia nobis
aptemus.   Dolus an virtus, quis in hoste requirat? 390
Arma dabunt ipsi.'   Sic fatus deinde comantem
Androgei galeam clipeique insigne decorum
induitur, laterique Argivum accommodat ensem.
Hoc Ripheus, hoc ipse Dymas, omnisque iuventus
laeta facit ; spoliis se quisque recentibus armat. 395
Vadimus immixti Danais haud numine nostro,
multaque per caecam congressi proelia noctem
conserimus ; multos Danaum demittimus Orco.
Diffugiunt alii ad navis, et litora cursu
fida petunt ; pars ingentem formidine turpi   400
scandunt rursus equum, et nota conduntur in alvo.

Coroebus, frenzied at seeing Cassandra a captive, leads the
company in an attempt to rescue her, and they are at the
same time assailed by fellow-Trojans, misled by their
Greek equipment

Heu! nihil invitis fas quemquam fidere divis!
Ecce trahebatur passis Priameia virgo
crinibus a templo Cassandra adytisque Minervae,
ad caelum tendens ardentia lumina frustra,   405

lumina, nam teneras arcebant vincula palmas.
Non tulit hanc speciem furiata mente Coroebus,
et sese medium iniecit periturus in agmen.
Consequimur cuncti et densis incurrimus armis.
Hic primum ex alto delubri culmine telis 410
nostrorum obruimur, oriturque miserrima caedes
armorum facie et Graiarum errore iubarum.
Tum Danai gemitu atque ereptae virginis ira
undique collecti invadunt, acerrimus Aiax,
et gemini Atridae, Dolopumque exercitus omnis : 415
adversi rupto ceu quondam turbine venti
confligunt, Zephyrusque, Notusque, et laetus Eoïs
Eurus equis : stridunt silvae, saevitque tridenti
spumeus atque imo Nereus ciet aequora fundo.
Illi etiam, si quos obscura nocte per umbram 420
fudimus insidiis, totaque agitavimus urbe,
adparent ; primi clipeos mentitaque tela
adgnoscunt, atque ora sono discordia signant.
Ilicet obruimur numero : primusque Coroebus
Peneleï dextra divae armipotentis ad aram 425
procumbit ; cadit et Ripheus, iustissimus unus
qui fuit in Teucris et servantissimus aequi.
Dis aliter visum. Pereunt Hypanisque Dymasque,
confixi a sociis, nec te tua plurima, Panthu,
labentem pietas, nec Apollinis infula texit. 430
Iliaci cineres, et flamma extrema meorum,
testor, in occasu vestro nec tela nec ullas

vitavisse vices Danaum, et si fata fuissent
ut caderem, meruisse manu.   Divellimur inde :
Iphitus et Pelias mecum, quorum Iphitus aevo   435
iam gravior, Pelias et vulnere tardus Ulixi ;
protinus ad sedes Priami clamore vocati.

*Aeneas, leading the few who survive, engages in the
defence of the royal palace*

Hic vero ingentem pugnam, ceu cetera nusquam
bella forent, nulli tota morerentur in urbe,
sic Martem indomitum, Danaosque ad tecta ruentis
cernimus, obsessumque acta testudine limen.   441
Haerent parietibus scalae, postisque sub ipsos
nituntur gradibus, clipeosque ad tela sinistris
protecti obiciunt, prensant fastigia dextris.
Dardanidae contra turris ac tecta domorum   445
culmina convellunt : his se, quando ultima cernunt,
extrema iam in morte parant defendere telis ;
auratasque trabes, veterum decora alta parentum,
devolvunt : alii strictis mucronibus imas
obsedere fores ; has servant agmine denso.   450
Instaurati animi regis succurrere tectis,
auxilioque levare viros, vimque addere victis.
   Limen erat caecaeque fores et pervius usus
tectorum inter se Priami, postesque relicti
a tergo, infelix qua se, dum regna manebant,   455
saepius Andromache ferre incomitata solebat

ad soceros, et avo puerum Astyanacta trahebat.
Evado ad summi fastigia culminis, unde
tela manu miseri iactabant inrita Teucri.   459
Turrim in praecipiti stantem summisque sub astra
eductam tectis, unde omnis Troia videri

ANDROMACHE, HOLDING HER CHILD ASTYANAX,
AND (RIGHT) HER HUSBAND HECTOR.
(From a vase of the 5th Century B.C., in the British Museum.)

et Danaum solitae naves et Achaica castra,
adgressi ferro circum, qua summa labantis
iuncturas tabulata dabant, convellimus altis
sedibus, impulimusque : ea lapsa repente ruinam 465
cum sonitu trahit, et Danaum super agmina late
incidit.   Ast alii subeunt ; nec saxa, nec ullum
telorum interea cessat genus.

Pyrrhus, son of Achilles, forces his way into the palace

Vestibulum ante ipsum primoque in limine Pyrrhus
exsultat, telis et luce coruscus aëna: 470
qualis ubi in lucem coluber mala gramina pastus,
frigida sub terra tumidum quem bruma tegebat,
nunc positis novus exuviis nitidusque iuventa,
lubrica convolvit sublato pectore terga
arduus ad solem, et linguis micat ore trisulcis.   475
Una ingens Periphas et equorum agitator Achillis,
armiger Automedon, una omnis Scyria pubes
succedunt tecto, et flammas ad culmina iactant.
Ipse inter primos correpta dura bipenni
limina perrumpit, postisque a cardine vellit   480
aeratos ; iamque excisa trabe firma cavavit
robora, et ingentem lato dedit ore fenestram.
Adparet domus intus, et atria longa patescunt ;
adparent Priami et veterum penetralia regum,
armatosque vident stantis in limine primo.   485
    At domus interior gemitu miseroque tumultu
miscetur ; penitusque cavae plangoribus aedes
femineis ululant ; ferit aurea sidera clamor.
Tum pavidae tectis matres ingentibus errant,
amplexaeque tenent postis, atque oscula figunt.   490
Instat vi patria Pyrrhus ; nec claustra, nec ipsi
custodes sufferre valent.   Labat ariete crebro
ianua, et emoti procumbunt cardine postes.

Fit via vi : rumpunt aditus, primosque trucidant
immissi Danai, et late loca milite complent.　　495
Non sic, aggeribus ruptis cum spumeus amnis
exiit, oppositasque evicit gurgite moles,
fertur in arva furens cumulo, camposque per omnis
cum stabulis armenta trahit.　Vidi ipse furentem
caede Neoptolemum, geminosque in limine Atridas ;
vidi Hecubam centumque nurus, Priamumque per
　　aras　　　　　　　501
sanguine foedantem quos ipse sacraverat ignis.
Quinquaginta illi thalami, spes tanta nepotum,
barbarico postes auro spoliisque superbi,
procubuere : tenent Danai, qua deficit ignis.　　505

*Priam, the aged king, prepares to resist, but is persuaded by
　his queen, Hecuba, to take refuge with her among the
　altars*

Forsitan et Priami fuerint quae fata, requiras.
Urbis uti captae casum convulsaque vidit
limina tectorum, et medium in penetralibus hostem,
arma diu senior desueta trementibus aevo
circumdat nequiquam umeris, et inutile ferrum　510
cingitur, ac densos fertur moriturus in hostis.
Aedibus in mediis nudoque sub aetheris axe
ingens ara fuit iuxtaque veterrima laurus,
incumbens arae atque umbra complexa penatis.
Hic Hecuba et natae nequiquam altaria circum,　515

praecipites atra ceu tempestate columbae,
condensae et divum amplexae simulacra sedebant.
Ipsum autem sumptis Priamum iuvenalibus armis
ut vidit, ' Quae mens tam dira, miserrime coniunx,
impulit his cingi telis?   Aut quo ruis? ' inquit.   520
' Non tali auxilio, nec defensoribus istis
tempus eget ; non, si ipse meus nunc adforet Hector.
Huc tandem concede ; haec ara tuebitur omnis,
aut moriere simul.'   Sic ore effata recepit
ad sese, et sacra longaevum in sede locavit.   525

*Polites, the son of Priam, is slain by Pyrrhus under his
    father's eyes ; and Priam, seeking to avenge his son, is
    likewise slain by Pyrrhus*

Ecce autem elapsus Pyrrhi de caede Polites,
unus natorum Priami, per tela, per hostis
porticibus longis fugit, et vacua atria lustrat
saucius.   Illum ardens infesto vulnere Pyrrhus
insequitur, iam iamque manu tenet et premit hasta.
Ut tandem ante oculos evasit et ora parentum,   531
concidit, ac multo vitam cum sanguine fudit.
Hic Priamus, quamquam in media iam morte tenetur,
non tamen abstinuit, nec voci iraeque pepercit.   534
' At tibi pro scelere,' exclamat, ' pro talibus ausis,
di, si qua est caelo pietas, quae talia curet,
persolvant grates dignas, et praemia reddant
debita, qui nati coram me cernere letum

'HAEC FINIS PRIAMI FATORUM.'

Pyrrhus with Polites & Priam, Menelaus & Helen left, Hecuba right and Hector's body below altar; from Athenian Cóth vase, Berlin.

fecisti, et patrios foedasti funere vultus.

At non ille, satum quo te mentiris, Achilles   540
talis in hoste fuit Priamo ; sed iura fidemque
supplicis erubuit, corpusque exsangue sepulcro
reddidit Hectoreum, meque in mea regna remisit.'
Sic fatus senior, telumque imbelle sine ictu
coniecit, rauco quod protinus aere repulsum,   545
et summo clipei nequiquam umbone pependit.
Cui Pyrrhus : 'Referes ergo haec, et nuntius ibis
Pelidae genitori : illi mea tristia facta
degeneremque Neoptolemum narrare memento.
Nunc morere.'   Hoc dicens, altaria ad ipsa tre-
        mentem   550
traxit et in multo lapsantem sanguine nati,
implicuitque comam laeva, dextraque coruscum
extulit ac lateri capulo tenus abdidit ensem.
Haec finis Priami fatorum ; hic exitus illum
sorte tulit, Troiam incensam et prolapsa videntem 555
Pergama, tot quondam populis terrisque superbum
regnatorem Asiae.   Iacet ingens litore truncus,
avulsumque umeris caput, et sine nomine corpus.

*Aeneas, catching sight of Helen, the cause of Troy's downfall,
        purposes to destroy her*

At me tum primum saevus circumstetit horror.
Obstupui ; subiit cari genitoris imago,   560
ut regem aequaevum crudeli vulnere vidi

vitam exhalantem ; subiit deserta Creüsa,
et direpta domus, et parvi casus Iuli.
Respicio, et quae sit me circum copia, lustro.
Deseruere omnes defessi, et corpora saltu   565
ad terram misere aut ignibus aegra dedere. ⌡

Iamque adeo super unus eram, cum limina Vestae
servantem et tacitam secreta in sede latentem
Tyndarida aspicio ; dant clara incendia lucem
erranti passimque oculos per cuncta ferenti.   570
Illa sibi infestos eversa ob Pergama Teucros,
et poenas Danaum et deserti coniugis iras
praemetuens, Troïae et patriae communis Erinys,
abdiderat sese, atque aris invisa sedebat.
Exarsere ignes animo ; subit ira cadentem   575
ulcisci patriam, et sceleratas sumere poenas :
' Scilicet haec Spartam incolumis patriasque Mycenas
aspiciet, partoque ibit regina triumpho?
Coniugiumque domumque patres natosque videbit,
Iliadum turba et Phrygiis comitata ministris?   580
Occiderit ferro Priamus? Troia arserit igni?
Dardanium toties sudarit sanguine litus?
Non ita. Namque, etsi nullum memorabile nomɩɛ
feminea in poena est nec habet victoria laudem,
exstinxisse nefas tamen et sumpsisse merentis   585
laudabor poenas, animumque explesse iuvabit
ultricis flammae, et cineres satiasse meorum.'

Venus, the mother of Aeneas, appears to him and directs him instead to save his father, wife and son

Talia iactabam, et furiata mente ferebar,
cum mihi se, non ante oculis tam clara, videndam
obtulit, et pura per noctem in luce refulsit   590
alma parens, confessa deam, qualisque videri
caelicolis et quanta solet ; dextraque prehensum
continuit, roseoque haec insuper addidit ore :
‘ Nate, quis indomitas tantus dolor excitat iras?
Quid furis?   Aut quonam nostri tibi cura recessit?
Non prius aspicies, ubi fessum aetate parentem   596
liqueris Anchisen?   Superet coniunxne Creüsa,
Ascaniusque puer?   Quos omnes undique Graiae
circum errant acies, et, ni mea cura resistat,
iam flammae tulerint inimicus et hauserit ensis. 600
Non tibi Tyndaridis facies invisa Lacaenae,
culpatusve Paris, divum inclementia, divum,
has evertit opes, sternitque a culmine Troiam.
Aspice : namque omnem, quae nunc obducta tuenti
mortalis hebetat visus tibi et umida circum   605
caligat, nubem eripiam : tu ne qua parentis
iussa time, neu praeceptis parere recusa.
Hic, ubi disiectas moles avulsaque saxis
saxa vides, mixtoque undantem pulvere fumum,
Neptunus muros magnoque emota tridenti   610
fundamenta quatit, totamque a sedibus urbem
eruit.   Hic Iuno Scaeas saevissima portas

prima tenet, sociumque furens a navibus agmen
ferro accincta vocat.
Iam summas arces Tritonia, respice, Pallas   615
insedit, nimbo effulgens et Gorgone saeva.
Ipse Pater Danais animos virisque secundas
sufficit ; ipse deos in Dardana suscitat arma.
Eripe, nate, fugam, finemque impone labori.
Nusquam abero, et tutum patrio te limine sistam.'
Dixerat ; et spissis noctis se condidit umbris.   621
Adparent dirae facies, inimicaque Troiae
numina magna deum.

*Aeneas goes in search of his father Anchises, who pleads age
and despair in support of his refusal to seek escape*

Tum vero omne mihi visum considere in ignis
Ilium, et ex imo verti Neptunia Troia ;   625
ac veluti summis antiquam in montibus ornum
cum ferro accisam crebrisque bipennibus instant
eruere agricolae certatim ; illa usque minatur
et tremefacta comam concusso vertice nutat,
vulneribus donec paulatim evicta supremum   630
congemuit traxitque iugis avulsa ruinam.
Descendo, ac ducente deo flammam inter et hostis
expedior ; dant tela locum, flammaeque recedunt.
Atque ubi iam patriae perventum ad limina sedis
antiquasque domos, genitor, quem tollere in altos 635
optabam primum montis primumque petebam,

abnegat excisa vitam producere Troia,
exsiliumque pati. ' Vos o, quibus integer aevi
sanguis,' ait, ' solidaeque suo stant robore vires,
vos agitate fugam.   **640**
Me si caelicolae voluissent ducere vitam,
has mihi servassent sedes. Satis una superque
vidimus excidia, et captae superavimus urbi.
Sic o sic positum adfati discedite corpus.
Ipse manu mortem inveniam : miserebitur hostis, **645**
exuviasque petet. Facilis iactura sepulcri.
Iam pridem invisus divis et inutilis annos
demoror, ex quo me divum pater atque hominum rex
fulminis adflavit ventis, et contigit igni.'

*Aeneas, in despair, resolves to throw himself once more
into the hopeless struggle against the Greeks*

Talia perstabat memorans, fixusque manebat.   **650**
Nos contra effusi lacrimis, coniunxque Creüsa
Ascaniusque omnisque domus, ne vertere secum
cuncta pater fatoque urgenti incumbere vellet.
Abnegat, inceptoque et sedibus haeret in isdem. **654**
Rursus in arma feror, mortemque miserrimus opto.
Nam quod consilium aut quae iam fortuna dabatur?
' Mene efferre pedem, genitor, te posse relicto
sperasti? Tantumque nefas patrio excidit ore?
Si nihil ex tanta superis placet urbe relinqui,
et sedet hoc animo, perituraeque addere Troiae   **660**

teque tuosque iuvat, patet isti ianua leto,
iamque aderit multo Priami de sanguine Pyrrhus,
gnatum ante ora patris, patrem qui obtruncat ad aras.
Hoc erat, alma parens, quod me per tela, per ignis
eripis, ut mediis hostem in penetralibus, utque   665
Ascanium patremque meum iuxtaque Creüsam
alterum in alterius mactatos sanguine cernam?
Arma, viri, ferte arma : vocat lux ultima victos.
Reddite me Danais ; sinite instaurata revisam
proelia. Numquam omnes hodie moriemur inulti.'670

Creusa pleads with Aeneas to give up his desperate resolve ;
and her pleas are reinforced by supernatural portents,
which move even Anchises

Hinc ferro accingor rursus, clipeoque sinistram
insertabam aptans, meque extra tecta ferebam.
Ecce autem complexa pedes in limine coniunx
haerebat, parvumque patri tendebat Iulum :
'Si periturus abis, et nos rape in omnia tecum ;   675
sin aliquam expertus sumptis spem ponis in armis,
hanc primum tutare domum. Cui parvus Iulus,
cui pater, et coniunx quondam tua dicta relinquor?'
    Talia vociferans gemitu tectum omne replebat ;
cum subitum dictuque oritur mirabile monstrum. 680
Namque manus inter maestorumque ora parentum
ecce levis summo de vertice visus Iuli
fundere lumen apex, tactuque innoxia mollis

lambere flamma comas, et circum tempora pasci.
Nos pavidi trepidare metu, crinemque flagrantem 685
excutere, et sanctos restinguere fontibus ignis.
At pater Anchises oculos ad sidera laetus
extulit, et caelo palmas cum voce tetendit :
' Iuppiter omnipotens, precibus si flecteris ullis,
aspice nos—hoc tantum—et, si pietate meremur, 690
da deinde auxilium, pater, atque haec omina firma.'

   Vix ea fatus erat senior, subitoque fragore
intonuit laevum, et de caelo lapsa per umbras
stella facem ducens multa cum luce cucurrit.
Illam, summa super labentem culmina tecti,   695
cernimus Idaea claram se condere silva,
signantemque vias ; tum longo limite sulcus
dat lucem, et late circum loca sulfure fumant.
Hic vero victus genitor se tollit ad auras,
adfaturque deos, et sanctum sidus adorat.   700
' Iam iam nulla mora est ; sequor, et qua ducitis,
    adsum.
Di patrii, servate domum, servate nepotem!
Vestrum hoc augurium, vestroque in numine Troia est.
Cedo equidem, nec, nate, tibi comes ire recuso.'

Aeneas, carrying his aged father and holding his son
by the hand, sets out in an attempt to escape

Dixerat ille ; et iam per moenia clarior ignis   705
auditur, propiusque aestus incendia volvunt.
' Ergo age, care pater, cervici imponere nostrae ;

ipse subibo umeris, nec me labor iste gravabit ;
quo res cumque cadent, unum et commune periclum,
una salus ambobus erit. Mihi parvus Iulus   710
sit comes, et longe servet vestigia coniunx.
Vos, famuli, quae dicam, animis advertite vestris.
Est urbe egressis tumulus templumque vetustum
desertae Cereris, iuxtaque antiqua cupressus,
religione patrum multos servata per annos :   715
hanc ex diverso sedem veniemus in unam.
Tu, genitor, cape sacra manu patriosque penatis :
me, bello e tanto digressum et caede recenti,
attrectare nefas, donec me flumine vivo
abluero.'   720
Haec fatus, latos umeros subiectaque colla
veste super fulvique insternor pelle leonis ;
succedoque oneri. Dextrae se parvus Iulus
implicuit, sequiturque patrem non passibus aequis :
pone subit coniunx. Ferimur per opaca locorum ; 725
et me, quem dudum non ulla iniecta movebant
tela, neque adverso glomerati ex agmine Grai,
nunc omnes terrent aurae, sonus excitat omnis
suspensum et pariter comitique onerique timentem.

*At the place appointed as a rendezvous Aeneas dis-
covers that his wife Creusa is missing*

Iamque propinquabam portis, omnemque videbar
evasisse viam, subito cum creber ad auris   731

visus adesse pedum sonitus, genitorque per umbram
prospiciens, ' Nate,' exclamat, ' fuge, nate ; pro-
   pinquant ;
ardentis clipeos atque aera micantia cerno.'
Hic mihi nescio quod trepido male numen amicum
confusam eripuit mentem.   Namque avia cursu 736
dum sequor, et nota excedo regione viarum,
heu! misero coniunx fatone erepta Creüsa
substitit ?   Erravitne via, seu lassa resedit ?
Incertum ; nec post oculis est reddita nostris.   740
Nec prius amissam respexi, animumve reflexi,
quam tumulum antiquae Cereris sedemque sacratam
venimus : hic demum collectis omnibus una
defuit, et comites natumque virumque fefellit.
Quem non incusavi amens hominumque deorumque?
Aut quid in eversa vidi crudelius urbe?   746
Ascanium Anchisenque patrem Teucrosque Penatis
commendo sociis, et curva valle recondo ;
ipse urbem repeto, et cingor fulgentibus armis.
Stat casus renovare omnis, omnemque reverti   750
per Troiam, et rursus caput obiectare periclis.

Returning to search for Creusa, Aeneas risks the lives of all
   his companions, till he is warned to desist by the phantom
   of Creusa herself

Principio muros obscuraque limina portae,
qua gressum extuleram, repeto ; et vestigia retro
observata sequor per noctem et lumine lustro.

Horror ubique animos, simul ipsa silentia terrent. 755
Inde domum, si forte pedem, si forte tulisset,
me refero. Inruerant Danai, et tectum omne tene-
    bant.
Ilicet ignis edax summa ad fastigia vento
volvitur ; exsuperant flammae ; furit aestus ad
    auras.
Procedo, et Priami sedes arcemque reviso.   760
Et iam porticibus vacuis Iunonis asylo
custodes lecti Phoenix et dirus Ulixes
praedam adservabant.   Huc undique Troia gaza
incensis erepta adytis mensaeque deorum
crateresque auro solidi captivaque vestis   765
congeritur.   Pueri et pavidae longo ordine matres
stant circum.
Ausus quin etiam voces iactare per umbram,
implevi clamore vias, maestusque Creüsam
nequiquam ingeminans iterumque iterumque
    vocavi.
Quaerenti et tectis urbis sine fine furenti   771
infelix simulacrum atque ipsius umbra Creüsae
visa mihi ante oculos, et nota maior imago.
Obstupui, steteruntque comae, et vox faucibus
    haesit.
Tum sic adfari, et curas his demere dictis :   775.
'Quid tantum insano iuvat indulgere dolori,
o dulcis coniunx? Non haec sine numine divum

eveniunt : nec te hinc comitem asportare Creüsam
fas aut ille sinit superi regnator Olympi.
Longa tibi exsilia, et vastum maris aequor arandum :
et terram Hesperiam venies, ubi Lydius arva   781
inter opima virum leni fluit agmine Thybris ;
illic res laetae regnumque et regia coniunx
parta tibi ; lacrimas dilectae pelle Creüsae.
Non ego Myrmidonum sedes Dolopumve superbas
aspiciam, aut Grais servitum matribus ibo,   786
Dardanis, et divae Veneris nurus :
sed me magna deum genetrix his detinet oris.
Iamque vale, et nati serva communis amorem.'
Haec ubi dicta dedit, lacrimantem et multa volentem
dicere deseruit, tenuisque recessit in auras.   791
ter conatus ibi collo dare bracchia circum ;
ter frustra comprensa manus effugit imago,
par levibus ventis, volucrique simillima somno.
Sic demum socios consumpta nocte reviso.   795

                       ⟵ End ⑤

Returning to his companions Aeneas finds that other fugi-
    tives have joined them, and together all make for the
    mountains

    Atque hic ingentem comitum adfluxisse novorum
invenio admirans numerum, matresque virosque,
collectam exsilio pubem, miserabile vulgus.
Undique convenere, animis opibusque parati,
in quascumque velim pelago deducere terras.   800

Iamque iugis summae surgebat Lucifer Idae,
ducebatque diem ; Danaique obsessa tenebant
limina portarum, nec spes opis ulla dabatur :
cessi, et sublato montis genitore petivi.'

'SUBLATO MONTIS GENITORE PETIVI.'
Aeneas sets out, carrying Anchises and holding Iulus
by the hand.   (Painted terracotta from Pompeii.)

NOTES

Line 1. **Conticuere :** for **conticuerunt,** 3rd pl. perf. indic. act. Notice this form, common in verse.

intentique ora tenebant, ' and eagerly fixed their eyes upon him ', *lit.,* ' and, attentive, held their faces '. Sometimes, as here, two stages are necessary in the translation of Vergil, first a bald, literal rendering, and then, after divining the meaning, a paraphrase in acceptable English idiom.

l. 2. pater : to Vergil, writing late in Roman history, it is natural to call Aeneas, legendary founder of his nation, ' father '.

orsus : supply **est.** The participle is from **ordior.**

l. 3. regina. The queen whom Aeneas is addressing is Dido of Carthage, to whose shores he has been driven by stress of weather.

l. 4. ut eruerint, an indirect question, hence the subjunctive. **ut =** ' how ', and is best prefaced by ' telling '.

l. 5. quaeque miserrima, ' and the most piteous things which '.

l. 6. et quorum . . . fui : ' of which I was a great part ' is unnatural in English. We should say rather, ' in which I took . . . '.

quis, ' which '.

talia fando, ' in saying such things,' i.e. ' in telling such a tale '. **fando** is ablative of the gerund of the deponent verb **for.**

l. 7. Myrmidonum Dolopumve. The Myrmidones were the warriors of Achilles, greatest soldier among the Greek enemies of Troy, and the Dolopes those of his son, Neoptolemus or Pyrrhus.

miles. With this word take **quis** of l. 6 again, rendering it this time ' what '.

Ulixi, gen. sg.　Ulysses, or Odysseus, was King of Ithaca, and celebrated among the Greek leaders for his craftiness and eloquence.

l. 8. **temperet, a** potential or conditional subjunctive : ' could refrain '.

caelo, ' from the heaven '.　The Roman poets frequently omit the prepositions which are necessary in prose to express place where, whither, whence.　In prose we should have **a caelo.**

l. 9. **cadentia,** ' setting '.　The meaning is that morning is at hand, and that it is high time to retire.

l. 10. **si tantus amor,** supply **est vobis** : ' if so great a desire is to you ', i.e. ' if you have so great a desire '.

casus, acc. pl.

l. 11. **laborem,** ' agony '.　The word means ' pain ' or 'trouble ' as often as it does ' work '.

l. 12. **luctu.**　Cf. the note on **caelo,** l. 8., and contrast **a lacrimis** in the same line.

l. 13. **fracti, repulsi** : the participles agree with **ductores.**

Danaum, gen. pl.　**-um,** the original gen. pl. ending of the 2nd declension, is often found in Latin poetry.

l. 14. **tot . . . annis,** ablative absolute, ' so many years now slipping by ', i.e. ' now that so many years were ', etc.

l. 15. **instar montis.**　So we too speak exaggeratingly of ' waves mountains high '.

Palladis.　The gods and goddesses took sides in the Trojan War.　From this we see that Pallas, worshipped especially at Athens, sided, naturally enough, with the Greeks.

l. 16. **sectaque,** etc., ' and interlace the ribs with planks of fir ', *lit.,* ' with sawn fir-wood '.　**intexunt** is poetical.　The meaning plainly is that a ' skeleton ' of stout timbers is

first made, and a ' skin ' of planks laid upon them afterwards.

l. 17. **votum ... simulant.** Supply **eum esse,** ' they pretend that it is ... '.

ea fama, ' that (is) the report (which) '.

l. 18. **Huc,** lit., ' hither ', =' in this ', i.e. the horse.

delecta ... corpora, ' having-chosen-by-lot (**sortiti**) picked
bodies of men '. Vergil means simply, ' having chosen certain men by lot.'

virum =gen. pl., see note on l. 13.

l. 19. **includunt.** Supply **eos** (=**viros**) as object.

caeco lateri, dat. after the compound verb **includunt,**
' within its dark flanks '. The phrase replaces the **in**
+ablative of prose. Notice **lateri,** sg. Vergil and the other
poets readily use sg. for pl., and vice versa, if metrical needs
call for it. **caecus** means properly ' blind ', but is often
used for other ideas connected with it, e.g. ' unseen ', ' pitch-
dark '.

ll. 19, 20. **cavernas ingentis uterumque.** We should say
' the vast recesses *of* the belly '. For the figure of speech,
(hendiadys) see note on l. 116. **Ingentis** is acc. pl., see
note on l. 40.

l. 20. **milite,** cf. note on **lateri,** l. 19.

l. 21. **Tenedos,** an island off the coast of Asia Minor, near
the entrance to the Dardanelles, on the southern shore of
which Troy stood. Consult the map.

fama, ablative.

l. 22. **opum,** ' in resources '. The genitive is similar to
those found with adjectives expressing fulness.

Priami. Priam was the King of Troy.

regna, pl. for sg. Contrast **lateri, milite** above.

l. 23. **tantum,** adverb, ' only '.

male fida. male here negatives, like the prefix in-. Translate ' fickle '. and cf. the French *mal*heureux, ' *un*happy '.

carinis. carina is ' keel ', but often used in poetry for
' ship '. The figure of speech, naming the part, but meaning the whole, is called *synecdoche.* ' Sail ' is used similarly
in English.

l. 24. **provecti,** lit. ' having been carried forth ' ; but the
passive of **veho** often means ' I carry myself ' = ' I go ',
' ride ', ' sail ', etc.

l. 25. The line is rather condensed. **rati** is for **rati sumus**
and **eos** must be supplied as subject to the two infinitives
in the acc. infin. construction. **rati** is from **reor.**

vento, abl., probably of the instrument. Translate ' with
a favourable wind '.

Mycenas. Mycenae, in the southern peninsula of Greece,
was the city of Agamemnon, chief among the princes of the
Greek host.

Teucria, ' Troyland '. Teucer was an ancient king of the
country.

l. 26. **luctu.** Notice once again the absence of the preposition usual in prose.

l. 27. **iuvat,** ' 'tis our delight ', *lit.,* ' it pleases (us) '.
Notice this second meaning of **iuvo,** ' I help '.

Dorica, ' Greek ' ; one of the divisions of the Greek race
was the Doric. Best known among the Dorians were the
people of Sparta.

l. 29. **hic,** adverb.

manus has a second meaning, employed here : ' band '
(of men). For **Dolopum** see note on l. 7.

tendebat, ' used to pitch his tent '. **tendo** means ' stretch ',
but is used intransitively here.

l. 30. **acie.** This time the missing preposition is **in.**

l. 31. **Pars.** Translate ' some ', and notice that Vergil
couples with the word, first a singular, then a plural verb.

exitiale, acc. sg. neuter of the adjective. Experience
shows that this is one of the last endings with which pupils
become familiar, and it is regularly taken as an adverb, or

as an ablative sg. Remember that the abl. sg. of 3rd decl. I-stem adjectives ends in -i.

l. 32. **primus hortatur,** ' is the first to urge ', the regular way of expressing such a meaning.

Thymoetes. The advice of this Trojan was perhaps traitorous, as he had a grudge against Priam.

l. 33. **duci,** pres. infin. pass. Supply **eum** and translate ' that it be led '. This acc. and infin. construction is Vergil's substitute for the usual **ut** and subj. after **hortor** and verbs of similar meaning.

arce. Supply **in.**

l. 34. **dolo,** ' out of treachery ', abl. of cause.

ferebant, ' tended ' ; **sic,** ' that way '.

l. 35. **et quorum . . . menti,** ' and (those) to the mind of whom (there was) a better opinion ', i.e. ' whose minds held better counsel '.

l. 36. **pelago,** a poetic dative for the **in pelagus** of prose.

l. 37. **praecipitare iubent,** ' bid hurl '. Contrast this transitive use of **praecipito** with that in l. 9.

subiectisve. **-ve,** attached to words in the same way as **-que,** =' or ', and is to be translated *before* the word to which it is attached.

l. 39. **studia,** ' factions '. The word means properly ' zeal ' ; here a group of people possessed with similar zeal.

l. 40. **omnis.** Note this, the better form of the acc. pl. of 3rd Declension I-stems.

magna, etc., abl. abs., ' with . . . '.

l. 41. **Laocoon** was a son of King Priam of Troy and his wife Hecuba. He was priest of Apollo.

ardens, translate as an adverb.

l. 42. **procul** : supply some such verb as **clamavit.**

quae tanta insania, supply **est haec.**

l. 43. **avectos,** supply **esse,** which is often omitted from the compound (fut. act. and perf. pass.) infinitives. See also note on l. 24.

hostis, acc. pl. Cf. note on **omnis,** l. 40.

l. 44. **dolis,** abl., governed by **carere,** which takes that case. **dolis** is an example of the pl. used for the sg. Contrast **lateri,** l. 19 ; **milite,** l. 20.

notus, supply **est vobis.** ' Is it thus Ulysses is known to you? ' meaning they should know that crafty leader better than to trust any gift of his.

l. 45. **hoc ligno,** ' by (but we should say ' in ') this woodwork '.

Achivi, one of the names for the Greeks, who are also variously called by Vergil **Graeci, Graii, Danai, Argivi, Argolici, Dorici, Pelasgi.** Similarly, among words for their enemies the Trojans, Vergil has **Troiani, Troii, Troes, Teucri, Dardanii, Iliaci, Dardanidae.**

l. 46. **in**+acc. sometimes, as here, expresses hostility : ' for the destruction of '.

l. 47. **inspectura, ventura.** The future participle is frequently used to express purpose : ' to spy on ', etc.

urbi, for the prose in **urbem.**

l. 48. **ne credite.** Again a poetic construction. In prose we should have **nolite credere.**

l. 49. A very famous line. **et dona ferentis,** ' even bringing (i.e. when they bring) gifts '. **ferentis** is acc. pl. again. Cf. note on **omnis,** l. 40.

l. 51. **curvam compagibus,** *lit.,* ' curved with timbers ', where we should say ' with its curved timbers '.

l. 52. **utero recusso,** probably abl. abs.

l. 54. **mens,** sc. **nostra,** ' our feelings '. **laeva,** here ' adverse ', is complement both to **fata** and **mens.** The meaning ' adverse ' derives from the fact that omens observed on the left hand (**laevus** = left) were regarded as portending ill.

l. 55. **impulerat,** ' he had compelled (us) ', pluperf. indic. instead of the usual pluperf. subjunctive, ' would have compelled '. It is suggested that the indic. conveys how narrowly Laocoon failed in his efforts to persuade the Trojans.

l. 56. **staret,** ' would be standing ', the usual meaning of the imperf. subj. in conditional sentences, assuming something which, at the moment of speaking, is contrary to the fact.

arx, vocative, as **maneres** shows.

l. 57. The skeleton (subj., vb., obj.) of the sentence is **pastores Dardanidae trahebant iuvenem. . . . revinctum.**

manus post terga revinctum, ' with his hands bound behind his back ', *lit.*, ' bound as to his hands ', etc. **manus** is acc. of respect or part concerned.

l. 59. **qui,** the antecedent of the relative is **iuvenem.**

se ignotum venientibus ultro . . . obtulerat, ' had of his own accord (**ultro**) put himself, a stranger (**ignotum**), in-their-path-as-they-advanced (**venientibus,** dat. after **obtulerat**).

l. 60. **strueret, aperiret,** final subjunctives, ' to . . . '.

l. 61. **animi,** locative.

in utrumque sc. **casum,** ' for either fate '.

l. 62. **versare dolos,** ' to practise his deceit '.

l. 63. **visendi studio,** ' in desire of seeing ', i.e. ' in their eagerness to see him '. **studio** is abl. of cause, and **visendi** is the gen. of the gerund.

iuventus, collective, but render ' young people '.

l. 64. **certant inludere,** ' vie to mock ', i.e. ' vie with one another in mocking '.

capto, dat. after the compound verb **inludere.** It is a masc. participle used as a noun.

l. 65. **crimine. ab uno.** The meaning is ' from the guilt of one man '.

l. 66. **omnis,** acc. pl.

l. 67. **ut** with the indicative always = ' as ' or ' when '.

medio, ' full '.

l. 68. **circumspexit** : note the spondee in the 5th foot.

l. 71. **cui . . . locus,** supply **est. cui** is ' for whom '.

et super. Take **cui** = ' from whom ', a second time after **et. super** is an adverb : ' moreover '.

l. 72. **poenas cum sanguine,** ' punishments with blood ', i.e. ' bloody punishment '.

l. 73. **quo.** In Latin often, only rarely in English, sentences begin with relatives, having antecedents in the previous sentences. Translate ' by this '.

conversi, sc. **sunt ; animi,** supply **nostri.**

compressus, sc. **est.**

l. 74. **Hortamur** : supply **eum** as obj.

fari, the infinitive here takes the place of the **ut** and subj. which is necessary in prose after **hortor** and practically all verbs of kindred meaning.

cretus, supply **sit.** Subjunctive in an indirect question, as are **ferat** and **sit** in the next line.

l. 75. **quid,** ' what (news) *or* (offer) '.

memoret, jussive subjunctive, ' let him say '. Observe that **memoro** does not mean ' I remember '.

quae . . . capto, supply **sit** and **sibi** : ' what confidence there is to him as a captive ', i.e. ' on what, as a prisoner, he relies ' (for hope of being spared ; that he has such a hope is to be inferred from his voluntary surrender).

l. 77. **cuncta vera,** ' all things true ', i.e. ' the whole truth '.

fuerit, fut. perf., ' shall come of it '.

l. 78. **me . . . negabo,** supply **esse.**

l. 79. **miserum** is predicative use of the adjective, as are **vanum** and **mendacem** in the next line. Translate them therefore *after* the object **Sinonem,** with which they agree.

Sinonem. This, of course, is the name of the spy.

l. 80. **finxit, finget.** In this line the verb **fingo** means ' make '.

l. 81. **fando,** ' in speech ', abl. of the gerund of the deponent verb **for.**

aliquod, adverbial acc., ' at all '. The literal meaning is ' any ', and those acquainted with the American vernacular will be familiar with such expressions as ' That won't help you any ', where also ' any ' = ' at all '.

auris, acc. pl.

l. 82. **Belidae Palamedis,** ' of Palamedes, son of Belus '.

fama is abl., and depends on **incluta** : ' and his renown, famous in story '.

l. 83. **quem,** etc. The order for translation is **quem Pelasgi demisere insontem neci. demisere** is for **demiserunt. neci** for the **ad necem** of prose.

falsa sub proditione is practically repeated by **infando indicio** : ' upon a false charge, the infamous allegation '.

l. 84. **quia,** ' that '.

bella, not ' wars ' in general, but ' the war ' which the Greeks were waging against Troy. Palamedes was slain for opposing it.

l. 85. Before **nunc** take **quem** again : ' but whom . . . '.

lumine, abl. of separation dependent on **cassum,** ' reft '. The phrase **cassum lumine** is a poetical way of saying ' dead '.

l. 86. **illi,** dat., best taken closely with **comitem** and **propinquum** : ' as his companion and kinsman ' (*lit.,* ' near by kinship ').

l. 87. **pauper** goes in grammar with **pater,** but is adverbial in sense : ' my father, being a poor man '.

in arma and **huc** are to be taken closely together : ' hither to war '.

l. 88. **stabat.** The subject is Palamedes.

regno, ' in his kingship ', goes with **incolumis.**

l. 89. **conciliis,** local abl. without preposition : ' in '.

et nos, ' I too '. The use of the plural pronoun instead of **ego** is frequent.

nomen, ' standing ', ' reputation '.

l. 90. invidia, abl. of cause : ' through the envy '.

postquam. Here, as very often, the best rendering is ' when '.

l. 91. ignota, acc. pl. neut.

concessit. The subject is still Palamedes.

superis ab oris, ' from the upper regions ', i.e. ' from the world above '.

l. 92. trahebam, ' dragged out '.

l. 93. mecum, ' within myself '.

l. 94. nec, ' but . . . not '.

demens gives the reason : ' in my madness '.

me subject to fore (to be supplied) in acc. and infin. construction dependent on promisi, l. 96 : ' vowed that I would be his avenger '.

qua, nom. sing. fem. of the *indefinite* adjective qui, ' any '.

tulisset, intransitive, ' offered '.

l. 95. remeassem (=remeavissem, a syncopated form) and tulisset, l. 94, subjunctive because they are the verbs of subordinate clauses in indirect speech. Sinon's own words were, ' ultor ero, si qua fors tulerit ' (fut. perf.).

l. 97. hino, ' from this cause '.

labes, ' taint '. With this word supply some such verb as ' came '.

hino—the second in the line—=' henceforth ', similarly in l. 98.

l. 98. terrere, spargere, and quaerere in l. 99 are what are called ' historic ' infinitives. These sometimes take the place of past tenses of the indicative, especially the imperfect, in descriptions of *repeated* action, and should be given the translation of such tenses.

voces, ' rumours '.

l. 99. conscius, adjective for adverb, ' guiltily '.

quaerere arma, ' sought arms ' means ' plotted violence '.

l. 100. **enim**, ' indeed ', an occasional meaning of the word.

Calchante ministro, abl. abs. ' with Calchas (as) his abettor '.

Calchas was a Greek soothsayer, a member of a profession to which any lack of scruple gives vast power among superstitious peoples.

l. 101. Here Sinon, having whetted the curiosity of his hearers, artfully breaks off with the equivalent of ' What's the good of telling you any more? '

quid, ' why ', a common meaning of the word. It has the same sense in l. 102.

haec ingrata revolvo, ' recount this unpleasing tale '.

nequiquam, ' in vain ', because, he implies, the attempt to arouse Trojan sympathy is bound to fail.

l. 102. **omnis**, acc. pl.

uno ordine habetis, *lit.*, ' you hold in one rank ', i.e. ' regard alike '.

l. 103. **id**, i.e. ' the name of Greek '.

l. 104. **Ithacus**, i.e. Ulysses, who was king of the island of Ithaca.

velit, mercentur, ' would wish ' and ' would buy ', conditional subjunctives, with the implied protasis, ' if they were to learn that I am in your hands '.

magno, abl. of price, ' at a great price '.

Atridae. The sons of Atreus were Agamemnon, chief leader of the Greeks, and his brother Menelaus.

l. 106. **scelerum**, ' knavery '.

l. 107. **pavitans**, with feigned—and no doubt some real—fear.

l. 108. **cupiere** = **cupiverunt**.

Troia relicta, abl. abs. But translate ' to leave Troy and . . . '.

l. 109. **fessi**, with **Danai**, and giving the reason for their desire to abandon the siege.

l. 110. **fecissent.** The pluperf. subjunctive, often, as here, accompanied by **utinam,** is used to express a wish that cannot be fulfilled, because the event has already ruled otherwise : ' would that they had done '.

ponti, ' upon the deep ' ; *lit.,* ' of '.

l. 111. **hiems,** sometimes, as here =' tempest '.

euntis, acc. pl., ' as they were on their way ', *lit.,* ' going '.

l. 112. **trabibus,** abl. of material with **contextus :** ' constructed of '.

l. 113. **toto aethere,** ' over the whole heaven '. The preposition is usually omitted from ' place ' phrases which include the word **totus.**

l. 114. **suspensi,** nom. pl. masc., and adj. for adv., ' anxiously '.

scitantem, ' to enquire '. The use of the pres. participle to express purpose is a variation of Vergil's for either **scitatum,** supine, or **scitaturum,** fut. partic.

l. 115. **adytis,** abl. of place whence without preposition.

l. 116. **placastis** =**placavistis** (syncopated form).

sanguine et virgine caesa, ' with blood *and* a slaughtered maid ', where we should say ' with the blood *of* a slaughtered maid '. The figure of speech, which consists in putting in the same case two nouns, one of which ought to depend upon the other in the genitive, is called hendiadys.

The ' slaughtered maid ' is Iphigeneia, daughter of Agamemnon, whom he was commanded to sacrifice, in order to secure favourable winds for the expedition against Troy.

l. 118. **quaerendi** and **litandum** are examples of the use of the gerundive expressing obligation : ' with blood your return is to be (=must be) sought, and with a Greek life you must win favourable omens.' **reditus** is poetic plural, and the verbs **sunt** and **est** must be supplied. For familiar examples of this use of the gerundive, cf. **Carthago est delenda,** ' Carthage must be destroyed ' (personal use), and **nunc est bibendum,** ' now's the time for drinking '.

l. 119. **quae**, ' this '. The relative after a full-stop is unusual in English.

vox, ' utterance '.

ut, ' when ', one of two meanings possible when the word is followed by the indicative. The other is ' as '.

auris, acc. pl. This form of the case should by now be familiar and will not in future be noticed.

l. 120. **obstipuere**, 3rd pl. perf. indic. act. This form, too, will not be noticed hereafter.

ima ossa, ' every part of their bodies ', *lit.*, ' inmost bones.'

l. 121. **parent, poscat**, subjunctives in indirect questions dependent on some such expression to be understood as this : ' as they asked themselves '.

l. 122. **hic**, adverb of time, ' at this '.

Ithacus, Ulysses.

Calchanta, acc. sg. of a Greek noun.

l. 123. **medios** agrees with **eos** understood, ' into their midst '.

numina, ' command ', pl. for sg.

l. 124. **canebant**. The verb means ' prophesy ' as well as ' sing '.

crudele, acc. sg. neut., agreeing with **scelus**. Note this 3rd decl. case ending, which often causes difficulty. Cf. l. 31.

l. 125. **taciti**. The participle is equivalent to a whole clause, ' though they said nothing '. **Canebant** then must mean that they prophesied in their own minds, and **mihi**, ' for me ', not ' to me '.

ventura, acc. pl. neut., ' the-about-to-come-things ', i.e. ' what was to come '.

l. 126. **quinos**. The numeral adjective **quini** belongs to the class called distributives, and means properly ' five each '. Here it is a variation for **quinque**.

ille, i.e. Calchas.

dies, acc. pl., expressing duration of time.

l. 127. **quemquam.** The word **quisquam**, ‘anyone’, is used only in sentences containing a negative, or some such virtual negative as **vix, aegre**, ‘ hardly ’, ‘ scarcely ’.

l. 129. **composito** shows that the reluctance of Calchas, suggested by **vix tandem**, l. 128, was merely simulated.

vocem must be translated ‘ silence ’ here.

ll. 130, 131. **quae sibi**, etc., ‘ bore (with equanimity) what each feared for himself (when it was) turned . . . ’.

l. 132. **parari**, historic infin. See note on **spargere**, l. 98.

l. 133. The **salsae fruges** and the **vittae** were usual accompaniments of sacrifice. The salted meal was sprinkled on the head of the victim, the fillet tied about its brows.

tempora. tempus here means ‘ temple ’ (of the head).

l. 134. **me**, acc.

l. 135. **lacu**, local ablative, ‘ by ’.

obscurus, ‘ hidden ’.

l. 136. **darent, dedissent.** The mood of these verbs is due to the fact that Sinon is reporting his own thoughts, or part of them, at the moment of hiding, and naturally they take the forms of indirect speech. In his own mind he said **dum vela dent** (final subjunctive, expressing his purpose in concealment, as well as a time-limit) **si forte dederint** (fut. perf.).

l. 137. **nec mihi (est) spes ulla**, ‘ nor to me is there any hope ’ = ‘ I have no hope ’. **mihi** is dative of the possessor.

l. 139. **quos**, ‘ from whom ’. **reposco**, like other verbs of *asking*, takes two accusatives.

illi, the Greeks.

et, ‘ too ’.

nostra, ‘ my ’. See note on **nos**, l. 89.

l. 141. **quod**, ‘ wherefore ’.

te, acc., object of **oro**, l. 143.

ll. 142, 143. **per si qua fides est quae restet**, *lit.*, ‘ by if any faith there-is which remains ’, i.e. ‘ by whatever faith is left '. restet is generic subjunctive, which is used in relative clauses having vague or indefinite antecedents.

l. 143. miserere, 2nd sg. imperative of the deponent misereor. Note that this form in the passive voice and in deponents is identical with the pres. infin. act.

laborum, ' troubles ', a very common meaning of the word.

l. 144. non digna ferentis, ' bearing not worthy things ', i.e. ' suffering undeservedly '.

l. 145. his lacrimis, abl. of cause, ' because of . . . '.

ultro, ' moreover '. ultro usually, as here, suggests going a step further than might have been expected. A good example of this is to be seen in l. 193.

ll. 146, 147. primus iubet, ' is the first to order ', the usual way of expressing this. Cf. note on l. 32.

l. 149. noster, ' ours ', i.e. ' one of us '.

mihique, etc., ' and speak true things to me asking these things ', i.e. ' answer these questions of mine truthfully '.

l. 150. quo, lit., ' whither ' =' to what purpose '.

molem . . . equi, ' this mass of a monstrous horse ', a way of saying ' this huge and monstrous horse '.

quis auctor, sc. erat. auctor =' begetter ', i.e. the man who prompted its construction.

l. 151. religio, ' act of duty to the gods '. Priam cannot decide whether the horse has a religious or military significance.

l. 152. dixerat, ' he had spoken ' =' he ceased '.

ille, i.e. Sinon.

instructus, ' ready '.

l. 154. vos. Sinon addresses the stars.

violabile. See note on crudele, l. 124.

l. 156. deum, gen. pl.

hostia, ' (as) victim '. Notice this very frequent need to supply ' as ' where Latin is content with simple apposition.

l. 157. fas, sc. est.

Graiorum, ' to the Greeks '. The genitive is open to a wide range of meanings, owing to the fact that this case is the only one used to express relations between one noun and another.

l. 158. **omnia ferre sub auras,** *lit.,* ' to bear everything up-into the air ', i.e. ' to bring everything to light '.

l. 159. qua, acc. pl. neut. of **quis,** *indefinite* pronoun.

patriae, gen.

l. 160. **promissis,** abl. of place, ' by . . . '.

maneas, serves, jussive subjunctives, equivalent in meaning to imperatives.

servata agrees with **Troia,** and gives Sinon's ground for the appeal **serves,** ' and having been (thyself) preserved '.

l. 161. **vera,** ' the truth '. This, or the neuter singular, is the regular way of translating ' truth ' when the meaning is ' the facts '.

feram, rependam, futures, which we must render in English by presents.

magna, acc. pl. neut. Sinon means ' if I pay back a great price '—for having been spared, of course. His suggestion is that the information he is about to give the Trojans (which is, we must remember, false and treacherous) will be full recompense for their clemency.

l. 162. **belli,** ' in the war ', objective genitive dependent on **fiducia.** See note on **Graiorum,** l. 157.

l. 163. **auxiliis,** pl. for sg., and local abl. ' stood (i.e. depended, rested) on the help '.

ex quo (sc. **tempore**), ' from the time when ', is balanced by **ex illo,** ' from that time ', l. 169. But **sed enim,** l. 164, must be taken first, and translated ' however '.

l. 164. **Tydides.** ' The son of Tydeus ' was Diomedes.

l. 165. **fatale.** See note on **crudele,** l. 124.

adgressi, in an unusual meaning, ' venturing '.

l. 166. **Palladium.** This was an image of Pallas, and according to Sinon, its sacrilegious seizure by Diomedes and Ulysses resulted in the loss to the Greeks of the goddess's help and support.

l. 168. **ausi = ausi sunt.** Similarly the appropriate parts of sum must be supplied with **fractae** and **aversa**, l. 170.

l. 169. **fluere** ('ebbed') and **referri**, historic infinitives. See note on **spargere**, l. 98. Here the historic infinitive expresses *continuity* of action.

sublapsa, 'gradually'. **labor**, 'glide' suggests motion not easily descried, and **sub**, adding the idea of 'slightly' or perhaps 'secretly', reinforces the notion.

l. 171. **nec** goes closely with **dubiis**, 'and with no uncertain . . .'. To say 'no uncertain' when 'certain' is meant is an instance of the figure of speech known as *litotes* or *meiosis*, in which deliberate understatement really gives additional emphasis.

ea signa, 'signs of this', the regular Latin for such an expression.

Tritonia, a name for Pallas.

l. 172. Rather condensed. 'Scarce (had) . . . been placed, (when). . . .'

castris. Another local ablative without preposition. This use should by now be familiar and will not always be noticed. There are two other examples, **luminibus and solo** (both place *whence*), in this sentence.

l. 173. **luminibus**, 'from the eyes', i.e. of the image. **lumen** is common in poetry in this sense.

per, 'down'.

l. 174. **iit**, 'ran'.

ipsa, i.e. the goddess.

mirabile dictu, 'marvellous to relate'. **dictu** is the supine in **-u**, properly an ablative of respect, 'in the telling'.

l. 175. The first **-que =** 'both'.

l. 176. **canit**, 'declares'.

aequora temptanda, with **esse** understood, acc. infin. after **canit,** ' that the sea must be braved '. **temptanda is** gerundive expressing obligation. Cf. l. 118.

fuga, abl., ' in flight '.

l. 177. **Pergama posse,** similarly dependent on **canit.**

l. 178. **ni is** for **nisi,** ' unless '.

omina repetant, ' seek omens anew ' (re-). Before the commencement of military operations, Roman generals sought to discover the attitude of the gods towards their designs by methods of divination, e.g. watching the flight of birds, inspecting the entrails of sacrificed victims, etc. This was called ' taking the auspices '. Calchas declares that the goodwill of Pallas has been lost, and can only be won by a fresh start from their home—Argos—and a new ' taking of the auspices '.

l. 179. **pelago et carinis,** ' *over* the sea and *in* their ships '.

l. 180. **quod,** ' as to the fact that '.

petiere = **petiverunt.**

l. 181. **comites,** ' (as) companions ', i.e. ' to accompany them '.

pelago remenso, abl. abs. **remenso** is from **remetior.**

l. 183. **moniti,** ' having been warned ', i.e. ' in consequence of a warning '.

l. 184. **quae piaret.** Relative clauses are often used in Latin to express adverbial, not adjectival, meanings. In such cases the verb is subjunctive. In the present instance the clause is one of purpose (final clause), **quae** = **ut ea,** and the best translation is ' to appease '.

l. 185. **immensam.** The adjective is intended to be taken after, and as expressing the result of the action of, the verb : ' raise *to a vast height* '. Such a use of the adjective is called *proleptic.* Cf. ' scrub the floor *clean* ', ' paint the walls *blue* '.

l. 186. **textis.** Not, of course, ' woven ', the usual meaning of the word, but perhaps ' interlaced ', or ' interlocking '.

caelo, poetic for ad caelum. Such poetical exaggeration is termed *hyperbole*.

iussit. Supply nos as object.

l. 187. portis would be per portas in prose.

dūcī, as the scansion shows, is pres. infin. pass. Contrast dŭcī (from dux).

possit, final subjunctive.

l. 188. tueri. Notice this word and its meaning, ' protect ', and beware of its chance resemblance to the French *tuer*.

ll. 189-194. violasset ... futurum (esse)'... ascendisset... venturam (esse) . . . manere. The subjunctives and infinitives of this passage report the words of Calchas indirectly, and represent his original future perfect, future and present indicatives, respectively. Begin : ' For, (said he) . . . '.

l. 189. dona Minervae, i.e. the horse.

ll. 190, 191. magnum exitium ... imperio... futurum, *lit.*, ' great ruin would be for the realm ', i.e. ' would befall . . . .'

l. 190. quod, relative adjective with omen.

di = dei.

ipsum, i.e. Calchas.

convertant, subjunctive expressing a wish (optative subjunctive). Translate ' may the gods turn . . . '.

l. 193. ultro, as before, implies ' going one better ' than expected. I.e. the Trojans will not only resist successfully —that might be expected—but will *actually* (ultro) carry the war into Greece.

Asiam, poetic for Troiam.

Pelopea. The adjective, which stands for ' Greek ', derives from Pelops, an ancestor of Agamemnon. Notice these ways of expressing, and yet avoiding, the plain unvarnished ' Troy ' and ' Greek '. For the Latin poets, it was the essence of poetry *not* to call a spade a spade.

l. 194. fata, pl. for sg., and subject of manere.

l. 195. **insidiis, arte,** abls. of cause, ' through . . . '.

l. 196. **credita,** sc. **est. res,** ' the tale '.

capti : supply **sumus,** and as subject, **nos,** antecedent to **quos,** ' and (we were) deceived . . . whom.'

l. 198. **anni decem,** i.e. the period of the siege.

l. 199. **hic,** temporal (i.e. ' time ') adverb. ' At this '.
The order for translation is **Hic aliud, maius multoque magis tremendum, obicitur (nobis) miseris.** Render **aliud** ' another incident '.

multo, abl. of the measure of difference, going as usual with a comparative, here **magis,** *lit.,* ' more dreadful by much '.

l. 201. **Lăŏcŏŏn,** 4 syllables.

ductus, ' chosen '.

l. 202. **sollemnĭs** : what case?

ad = ' at '.

l. 203. **a Tenedo.** The preposition would be omitted in the best prose, Tenedos being an island small enough to be considered as one place.

alta, adj. used as noun, ' depths ', or ' deep '.

l. 205. **incumbunt** (+ dat.), ' breast '.

l. 206. **quorum.** The Latin relative, occurring after a stop other than a comma, should be translated by a personal or demonstrative pronoun, as required—in this case ' their '.

l. 207. **sanguineae,** ' blood-red '.

pars cetera, i.e. the body and tail.

l. 208. **pone,** adverb.

sinuatque, etc., ' and curves the endless coils of the back ', *lit.,* ' the endless back with its coil '. The expression, while easy enough to understand, as a description of the alternate raising and depression of the serpents' coils as they ' undulate ' over the surface of the sea, is made awkward by the fact that **pars cetera** is the subject (and thus the back is described as curving the back) and by the ill-attached volumine. Vergil might have written **immensa volumina tergi**, but it is characteristic of him to avoid the obvious.

l. 209. **spumante salo**, abl. abs., to be rendered by a clause, ' as the salt sea foamed '.

tenebant, *lit.*, ' held ', i.e. ' had reached '.

l. 210. ' and, their blazing eyes suffused with blood and fire ' ; *lit.*, ' suffused as to their blazing eyes '. **oculos** is the accusative of respect or part concerned. Cf. note on **manus**, l. 57.

l. 212. **visu**, abl. of cause, modifying **exsangues**.

agmine cerʻo, abl. of manner. Render **agmen** by ' course '. **certo** expresses the purposeful advance of the serpents, ' unswerving '.

l. 213. **Laocoonta**, acc. sg. of a Greek noun.

l. 214. **corpora**, acc. pl., object of **amplexus**.

amplexus. The perfect participles of deponent verbs **may** be used in a present meaning.

l. 215. **morsu depascitur**, *lit.*, ' feeds upon with biting ', i.e. ' devours '.

l. 216. **post**, adverb.

ipsum, i.e. Laocoon.

auxilio, ' to their assistance '. This **is the dative** of purpose, found in the case of the nouns **auxilium, subsidium** (' support ') and **praesidium** (' protection '), and in association with verbs of motion, or with **relinquo**.

l. 218. **medium**, ' his middle '.

ll. 218, 219. **circumdati**, from **circumdo**, is written as two separate words. The passive participle has an active meaning here, ' having put . . . round his neck '. Latin poets occasionally give the passive voice an active sense, in imitation of the Greek *middle* voice, which, while having most of its forms identical with those of the passive, expresses active action done *to* or *for* oneself.

l. 219. **terga**, ' bodies '.

ll. 220, 222. simul ... simul. Translate the first by ' while ', the second by ' at the same time '.

l. 221. perfusus vittas, same construction as **suffecti oculos,** l. 210. *Lit.,* ' drenched as to his fillets ', i.e. ' his fillets drenched '.

sanie, veneno, i.e. his own blood and the serpents' venom.

l. 223. qualis mugitus, ' like the bellowing '.

fugit, perfect, as the scansion shows.

l. 224. incertam, 'ill-aimed '. The bull is gravely wounded, but not killed.

securim, one of a class of nouns with acc. in -im, abl. sg. in -i. Others are **turris,** ' tower '; **puppis,** ' stern of a ship '; **tussis,** ' cough '.

l. 225. lapsu, abl. of manner, ' by gliding '. —Render ' gliding away '.

l. 226. Tritonidis, i.e. of Pallas (Minerva), who had sent them to remove Laocoon, he having shown (ll. 40, 41) an attitude of suspicion calculated to wreck the plans of the goddess.

l. 227. teguntur, ' are hidden ' = ' hide themselves '. In Latin the passive voice is often an alternative for the active + the acc. of the reflexive pronoun.

l. 228. cunctis, ' of all ', the dative being very frequently used in Latin where a possessive genitive would be natural in English.

l. 229. insinuat, used intransitively, ' steals '.

merentem, adj. for adv., ' deservedly '.

l. 230. ferunt, ' (men) say ', with **Laocoonta expendisse,** acc. and infin., dependent on it.

ll. 230, 231. qui laeserit ... intorserit, an adverbial relative clause, this time of cause, ' in that he ... '. Cf. note on l. 184.

l. 232. ducendum, oranda, ' must be led ', ' must be entreated '. Gerundives, used personally, i.e. in agreement

with the nouns **simulacrum** and **numina** respectively, expressing obligation. The whole sentence **ducendum** ...
numina is acc. and infin. dependent on **conclamant**, and **esse** must be supplied.

l. 235. **accingunt**, ' gird themselves '. Vergil is using this verb without its object, **se**.

ll. 235, 236. **rotarum lapsus**, ' glidings of wheels ', a Vergilian variation for ' gliding wheels ', or ' rollers '.

l. 237. **intendunt**, ' stretch ', or ' lead ', as a preliminary to hauling.

l. 238. **circum**, adverb.

l. 239. **sacra**, ' sacred things ', i.e. ' hymns '.

l. 241. **domus**, in apposition with **Ilium**.

divum, gen. pl.

l. 244. **furore**, abl. of cause explaining **caeci**, i.e. ' in our madness '.

l. 245. **infelix**, acc. sg. neut.

l. 246. **fatis futuris**, dat., *lit.*, ' for the fates to be ', i.e. ' to foretell the future '.

Cassandra, a daughter of King Priam of Troy ; she possessed the gift of prophecy.

l. 247. **ora**. The plural of **os**, ' mouth ', may often be translated ' lips '.

dei, ' of heaven '. Sometimes, as here, no particular god is meant.

Teucris, ' by the Trojans ', dative of the agent, often found in poetry instead of ab + ablative.

l. 248. **esset**, subjunctive in an adverbial relative clause, with concessive meaning. ' Though that day ', etc. See l. 184 for a final example, and ll. 231, 232 for an instance of **qui** causal.

l. 250. **vertitur**, ' turns ' or ' revolves ', the passive being equivalent to an intransitive active. It seems to have been thought that the alternation of light and darkness was due rather to a movement of the sky than to a revolving earth.

l. 252. fusi, from **fundo,** ' I pour ', suggests the abandon of a fatigued sleep. Translate ' out-stretched '.

l. 254. phalanx, properly a particular military formation, is loosely used for ' host '.

l. 255. a Tenedo. Cf. note on l. 203.

amica, ' friendly ', that is, to the Greeks.

l. 256. flammas, i.e. a ' fire-signal ', no doubt hoisted to the mast-head in a brazier.

puppis, an instance of synecdoche, i.e. the naming of the part instead of the whole. Thus **puppis** = ' ship '. Cf. **carinis** and note, l. 23.

l. 257. extulerat. The pluperfect is sometimes used to express suddenness of action : ' hoisted '. The indicative is usual in what are called *inverse* **cum** clauses.

l. 259. laxat, ' releases ', has two objects, the second of which, **pinea claustra,** should really come first.

auras, *lit.*, ' breezes ', often used for ' air ' or ' light '.

l. 262. lapsi, ' sliding '. Cf. note on **amplexus,** l. 214.

per, ' down '.

l. 263. primus, probably rather ' chieftain ' than ' first ', as Machaon is mentioned so late.

vino. Plainly the Trojans had indulged in a carouse in their relief at the raising of the siege.

l. 266. patentibus, ' through the open gates ', abl. of route.

l. 268. quo, ' at which ', abl. of time when.

aegris, ' weary ', rather than ' sick '.

l. 269. serpit, i.e. ' steals *over them* '.

l. 270. Hector, son of Priam, and chief warrior of the Trojans. Slain by Achilles, he was dragged round the walls of Troy behind the victor's chariot, as mentioned in ll. 270, 271.

l. 271. visus, sc. **est.**

adesse mihi, ' to be present to me ', i.e. ' to stand at my side '.

fletus, acc. pl., *lit.*, ' weepings ', =' tears '.

l. 272. **raptatus,** *lit.*, ' having been dragged '. The meaning is that the vision of Hector seen by Aeneas had all the appearance of having been freshly dragged by the chariot.

bigis, abl., with **raptatus.**

ut quondam, ' as once *he was* '.

l. 273. **traiectus lora.** This is a difficult instance of that extension of the use of the passive of which simpler examples have been noted before. Grammatically Vergil should have written **traiectus pedes loris,** ' pierced as to the feet with thongs '. In any case the translation is ' his feet pierced with thongs '—for the dragging, of course. **tumentis,** ' swollen ' is acc. pl. and goes with **pedes.**

l. 274. **qualis erat,** *lit.*, ' of what sort he was ', i.e. ' how he looked ! '

l. 275. **redit,** historic present.

indutus, middle use of the passive voice, i.e. having active and indirectly reflexive meaning, ' having put on himself '. Translate ' clad in ', and cf. note on **circumdati,** l. 219.

exuvias Achilli. These ' spoils of Achilles ' were taken by Hector from the body of Patroclus, who had borrowed his friend's armour.

l. 276. **iaculatus,** ' after hurling ', *lit.*, ' having hurled '.

puppibus, poetic dat. in place of **in** + acc. See also note on this word, l. 256. The allusion is to an attempt by the Trojans under Hector to fire the Greek fleet.

l. 277. **barbam, crinis, vulnera,** objects of **gerens.**

l. 278. **plurima,** agreeing with **quae,** ' in great number '.

l. 279. **ultro** has more or less its usual meaning, i.e. whereas Hector's apparition might have been expected to speak first, it is actually Aeneas who does so. Translate ' first '.

videbar, in its very common deponent meaning ' seemed '.

l. 280. **voces,** ' words ', as often in poetry.

l. 282. **morae**, pl. for sg. **tantae**, ' long ' merely.

l. 283. **exspectate**, voc. sg. masc., ' O long awaited H. '
ut, exclamatory, ' how *gladly* '.

l. 284. **funera**, ' deaths ', *lit.*, ' funerals '.

labores, ' tribulations ', as so commonly.

l. 285. **defessi**, nom., ' we weary ones '.

indigna, ' shameful '.

l. 287. **nihil**, sc. **respondit**.

me quaerentem vana, ' me seeking vain things ', i.e. ' my
vain questionings '.

moratur, usually intransitive, ' tarries ', here =' tarries
for ', i.e. ' heeds '.

l. 289. **nate dea**. **nate** is voc., **dea** abl., ' thou-having-
been-born from a goddess ', i.e. ' goddess-born '. **dea** is
abl. of origin.

l. 291. **datum**, sc. **est a te**.

Pergama, nom. pl. neut., is the name of the citadel of
Troy, and so stands here for ' Troy ' itself.

dextra, *lit.*, ' by a right hand ', i.e. ' by any man's hand '.

l. 292. **possent, fuissent,** subjunctives in a conditional
sentence containing an assumption about the past which is
contradicted by the fact of the present : ' could have ' . . .
' would have '.

l. 294. **comites**, ' *as* companions '. This use of simple
apposition where English prefers to insert ' as ' has been
noted before, l. 156.

fatorum, i.e. ' of your destiny '.

his, abl., ' with *the aid of* these '.

l. 295. **magna**, with **moenia**, which is the antecedent of
quae.

pererrato ponto, abl. abs., ' when . . . '.

l. 296. Vesta was the Roman goddess of fire. Vergil's
object is to suggest that Roman religion had its origins in
Troy. In thus seeking to dignify Rome by associating its

beginnings with the great body of legend enshrined in Homer, Vergil is following an ancient Latin tradition, already elaborated by earlier Latin writers. The reference to **Penatis**, l. 293, is similar in purpose, for these were ancient Roman gods of the store cupboard and the household.

l. 297. **penetralibus,** here an adj., ' inmost '.

l. 298. A Vergilian way of saying : ' the walls are echoing with confused cries of grief '.

l. 299. **secreta,** supply **est.**

l. 300. **Anchisae.** Anchises was the father of Aeneas.

recessit, *lit.,* ' has gone back ', =' lay back ' (i.e. from other houses).

l. 301. **armorum,** ' battle '.

horror, ' the terrifying din '.

l. 302. **excutior** is another instance of the passive voice used as an equivalent for active + reflexive pronoun.

summi fastigia tecti. The sense is plainly ' the roof top of the house ', though Vergil, with his usual avoidance of the obvious, says ' roof of the house top '.

l. 303. **supero,** ' reach '.

l. 304. **veluti cum** introduces a simile : ' even as when '.

l. 306. **sata,** acc. pl. neut., perf. partic. pass. of **sero,** ' I sow ', and therefore =' crops '.

laeta, ' heartening ', since of course the word expresses not the joyousness of the crops, but the effect upon the beholder of seeing them. This is an example of ' transferred epithet ' or hypallage. The expression ' joyous crops ', occurring in English poetry, would similarly be acceptable and natural.

boum labores. ' The labours of oxen ' is simply a way of saying ' crops ' over again, since the necessary ploughing had first to be done by them.

l. 307. **inscius,** ' ignorant *of the cause* '.

l. 309. **fides,** ' truth '. Supply **est.**

l. 310. **Deiphobi,** another of Priam's sons.

l. 311. **Vulcano,** ' fire ', the name of the god of fire being used for the thing itself, a very common poetic idiom, of which other examples are **Bacchus** for ' wine ' and **Ceres** for ' bread '. **superante,** with **Vulcano** in the abl. abs., ' gaining the mastery '.

l. 312. **Ucalegon,** i.e. ' Ucalegon's house '.

Sigea. ' The Sigean sea ' washes the Mediterranean coast of Asia Minor immediately S. of Gallipoli, Sigeum being the name of a cape. It is thus the sea to the W. of Troy.

l. 314. **nec sat rationis,** etc. The sense is ' yet without clear purpose ', *lit.,* ' nor (is there) enough of reason '.

l. 316. **ardent,** ' is eager ' ; **animi,** nom. pl. for sg.

l. 317. **pulchrumque,** etc., ' and it occurs (to me) that it is noble '.

l. 320. **deos,** their images, of course.

l. 321. **ad limina,** ' to *my* door '. **limen,** properly ' threshold ', is an example of synecdoche.

l. 322. **res summa,** i.e. ' the hardest fighting '. Supply **est.**

Panthu, voc.

l. 323. **talia,** ' such *words as these* '.

l. 325. **fuimus,** ' have been ' =' are no more '. **fuit** similarly.

l. 326. **Argos,** acc. pl., the name of the town, without any preposition, expressing the place towards which, the goal of motion : ' to Argos '. Argos, a city in the Peloponnese, is selected as a symbol for ' Greece '.

l. 329. **miscet,** ' spreads '.

l. 331. **milia quot,** ' as many thousands as '.

ll. 332, 333. **telis oppositis,** ' with weapons placed-in-the-way ', i.e. ' with a fence of spears '.

l. 332. **angusta viarum,** 'narrows of the ways', a Vergilian expression for 'narrow ways'. Cf. **rotarum lapsus,** ll. 235, 236.

l. 333. **stat, etc.** Either ' there stands a line of steel, with flashing points drawn ', in which case **stricta,** in a manner quite typical of Vergil, goes in grammar with **acies,** in sense with **mucrone ;** or, more obvious, if less effective, ' their blades of steel stand drawn, with flashing points '. **acies** means (i) edge of a sword or similar implement, (ii) (by a metaphor), a straight line of armed men.

l. 334. **neci,** for ' death ', i.e. ' to deal death '.

l. 335. **caeco Marte. Mars** =' war ' exactly as **Vulcanus,** l. 311, =' fire '. **caecus,** either because all is dark, or, better, because their resistance is undirected and without real knowledge of their position.

l. 337. **feror** =**fero me,** i.e. ' I go ', or 'rush'.

quo, adv.

Erinys, ' the Fury '. The Furies, three goddesses of ancient mythology, were punishers of human wrongdoing, and might be supposed to rejoice in such a scene of carnage. **tristis,** ' grim '.

l. 338. **aethera,** acc. sg. of **aether,** a Greek noun.

l. 339. **addunt se socios,** ' add themselves *as* comrades ', i.e. ' join me '. For the regular omission of ' as ' cf. **comites,** l. 294 and note.

l. 340. **oblati,** ' having been brought in my way ', i.e. ' meeting me '.

l. 341. **adglomerant.** The object is **se,** repeated from l. 339.

nostro = **meo.** This is common in poetry.

l. 342. **ad Troiam. Troiam** in prose.

l. 343. **Cassandrae** is objective genitive, i.e. it bears the same relation to the noun **amore** as would an object, **Cassandram,** to the verb **amo.** We must, however, translate ' for Cassandra '. The latter was a daughter of Priam.

l. 344. gener, ' *as his* son-in-law *to be* '. For the ' as ' see note on **comites,** l. 294, and cf. **socios,** l. 339.

l. 345.   **qui** = ' in that he ', as the subjunctive **audierit,** (causal) shows.   Remember that relative pronouns are often used to introduce adverbial clauses of various types and that in such clauses the subjunctive is always used.

furentis, not ' raving ' but ' inspired '.   Cassandra had foretold the doom of Troy (l. 246).

l. 347. **quos,** ' that they ', subject to the infin. **audere.** There have been several previous instances of the use of a relative at the beginning of a new sentence.

audere in proelia, ' were bold for battle '.

l. 348. **super,** adv., ' further ', i.e. observing that his companions are in good heart, he yet proceeds to rouse them further.

his, sc. **verbis.**

l. 349. **vobis,** sc. **est,** = ' you have '.   In this case the subject of **est, cupido,** will become object of ' have '.

audentem extrema, ' me in my last venture '.   **audentem** agrees with **me** understood and **extrema** is acc. pl. neut. of the adj.—*lit.,* ' *me* daring the last things '.

l. 350. **sit,** subjunctive in an indirect question, ' what fortune there is to our affairs ', i.e. ' how ill our affairs are going '.

l. 35ᴛ. **relictis,** with **adytis** and **aris** in the abl. abs. construction ; translate ' leaving their shrines and altars '.

l. 352. **quibus,** ' by whose support '.

steterat, ' *once* stood '.   The pluperfect emphasizes the finality of the gods' desertion.

l. 353. **moriamur ... ruamus.**   The subjunctives are hortative, ' let us ... '.   Actually the verbs should be in reverse order, but the difficulty can be met by rendering **ruamus** by a participle, ' rushing '.

arma, ' fray ', as often in poetry.

l. 354. **salus,** supply **est.**

l. 355. **furor,** ' desperation ' ; **additus, sc. est.**

l. 356. **raptores,** adjectivally, ' ravening '.

ventris, ' of their bellies ', i.e. ' of famine '.

l. 357. **caecos,** render as adverb, ' blindly ', i.e. with reckless disregard of danger.

catulique. Before this clause repeat **quos** : ' and which '.

l. 358. **siccis,** i.e. unmoistened by the blood of prey.

l. 359. **haud dubiam,** *litotes,* =' certain '.

ll. 359, 360. **mediaeque** . . . **iter,** plainly =' hold our course through the centre of the city ', though the expression, as often in Vergil, defies literal translation.

l. 360. **cava** is ablative, as the scansion shows.

l. 361. **funera,** ' deaths ', as before.

fando, abl. of the gerund of **for.** Cf. l. 6.

l. 362. **explicet,** ' potential ' subjunctive (i.e. conditional with ' if ' clause suppressed), ' could unfold '.

labores, ' woes '.

ll. 364, 365. **per,** ' about '.

l. 366. **limina,** same meaning as in l. 321.

l. 367. **victis,** dative in place of a possessive genitive, common in Latin.

l. 369. **luctus, sc. est.**

plurima mortis imago, ' very many a form of death ', Vergilian for ' death in countless forms '.

l. 370. **comitante caterva,** abl. abs., best rendered by a passive participle, attended by a throng.' *Lit.,* ' a throng attending '.

l. 371. **socia agmina.** Supply **nos esse;** all four words are in the acc. and infin. construction, depending on **credens.**

l. 372. **inscius,** adverbially, ' in his ignorance '.

amicis, adjectival, ' friendly '.

l. 373. **sera,** ' laggard '. **tam** is untranslatable.

l. 374. **rapiunt feruntque,** ' harry and plunder '.

incensa, ' kindled ', and so ' flaming '.

l. 375. **celsis.** We too speak of ' tall ships '.

primum, ' for the first time '.

itis, where we should expect **venitis.**

l. 376. **neque.** Translate as if **nulla.**

l. 377. **sensit delapsus** = **sensit se delapsum esse.** This is an imitation of the Greek idiom whereby verbs of perceiving are followed by acc. and participle, and by the participle alone, in the nom. case, if the subject of the indirect statement is the same as that of the ' perceiving ' verb.

l. 378. **retro,** almost superfluous.

pedem cum voce. We should say ' voice and step '.

l. 379. **veluti,** ' even as ', introducing a simile, as the same word does in l. 304. **qui,** (one) who '.

improvisum. We should say rather ' unawares '. Grammatically of course it goes with **anguem** and means ' not previously seen '.

aspris = **asperis,** and is shortened for metrical convenience.

sentibus, place where, ' among brambles '.

l. 380. **pressit.** The subject, not expressed, is indefinite : ' one '.

nitens, ' treading hard '.

l. 381. **attollentem** and **tumentem** agree with **eum** (= **anguem**) understood. **eum** is the object of **refugit.**

attollentem iras, ' raising its wrath ', Vergilian for ' rising in wrath '.

tumentem is best translated as a transitive verb with **colla** as its object. Actually it is an intransitive verb, and **colla** is acc. of respect : ' swelling as to its neck '.

l. 382. **abibat,** what is called the conative use of the imperfect, i.e. imperfect expressing attempted action : ' sought to withdraw '.

l. 383. **circumfundimur** = **nos** (reflexive) **circumfundimus,** ' we pour ourselves around ', i.e. ' surround them '.

l. 384. **ignaros** and **captos** agree with **eos** understood, object of **sternimus.**

l. 385. **Adspirat.** The English idiom would be ' smiles upon '. The literal, ' breathes upon ', is of course a metaphor from sailing, fortune being compared to a favouring wind.

l. 386. **hic,** temporal adverb.

l. 387. **qua,** adverb.

l. 388. **dextra,** ' propitious'. **Dextram,** in agreement with se, would have been more natural. **dexter** and **sinister,** ' right ' and ' left ', are also ' lucky ' and ' unlucky ', according to the convention of Roman divination, i.e. the interpreting of omens. See note on **laeva,** l. 54.

sequamur, hortative subjunctive, ' let . . . '. Similarly **mutemus** and **aptemus,** in the succeeding lines.

l. 390. **Dolus an virtus,** condensed for **utrum sit dolus an virtus,** alternative indirect question dependent on **requirat.**

in hoste, ' among the foe ', i.e. ' surrounded by foes '. The sense is that men in so perilous a situation as theirs is can take no account of the ethics of the course proposed.

requirat, potential, ' would ask '.

l. 392. **clipei insigne decorum,** ' the fair device of the shield ', Vergilian for ' his shield, with the beautiful device upon it '.

l. 393. **induitur,** ' puts upon himself ', a very good example of the *middle* use of the passive voice, explained in the note on l. 218.

l. 395. **laeta,** adj. for adv.

l. 396. **immixti,** middle and present in meaning, ' mingling '. **Danais,** dative, depends on it.

haud numine nostro, ' under gods not our own ', as if the wearing of Greek armour gave them the protection of a different set of divinities.

l. 398. **conserimus,** *lit.,* ' join ', with **proelia** as object, but best translated ' fight '.

Orco, poetic dative of place whither—**ad Orcum** in prose.

ll. 399, 400. **litora fida,** ' trusty shores ', i.e. ' safety of the shores '.

l. 400. **pars,** a variation for **alii,** as the plural verb with it (**scandunt**) shows.

formidine, abl. of manner, ' in . . . '.

l. 401. **conduntur = condunt se,** as often.

l. 402. **nihil,** etc. *Lit.,* ' (it is) right that anyone should trust the unwilling gods in nothing ', i.e. ' it is not right that one should trust the gods in aught, against their will '. **nihil** is adverbial accusative.

l. 403. **passis,** from **pando,** ' dishevelled '.

Priameia, ' daughter of Priam '.

l. 404. **Cassandra.** She had been betrothed to Coroebus, and the sight of her thus treated naturally fired him to a piece of recklessness which ruined his comrades.

l. 405. **tendens,** ' straining '.

l. 406. **palmas,** synecdoche, ' hands '.

l. 408. **periturus,** ' to die ', the future participle expressing not purpose, as it often does, but the inevitable result of his action.

l. 410. **hic,** adverb.

l. 411. **nostrorum,** ' of our own men '.

obruimur. The last syllable is, irregularly, long.

l. 412. **facie** and **errore** are ablatives of cause. ' owing to '. **error,** ' mistaking '.

l. 413. **gemitu atque ira,** *lit.* ' with a cry and in anger (at) . . . ', where we should say, ' with a roar of anger ', etc. **gemitus** usually means a cry of grief or pain.

ereptae virginis, ' at the maiden rescued ', where we prefer, ' at the maiden's rescue '. Cassandra had been temporarily snatched from her captors.

l. 414. **acerrimus,** supply **omnium.**

l. 415. **Atridae,** see note, l. 104.

l. 416. **rupto turbine,** 'when a storm breaks'. Notice
that the *passive* voice of **rumpo** is required to translate the
English intransitive ' break '.

i. 417. **Zephyrus, Notus, Eurus** are the Greek names for
the West, South and East winds.

l. 418. **equis.** The winds are imagined as chariots drawn
by teams of horses, the whole picture suggesting force and
speed.

tridenti—the usual weapon of all the gods of the sea.

l. 419. **Nereus,** a sea-god, son of Oceanus and Tethys.

l. 420. **Illi . . . si quos,** *lit.,* ' those . . . if any ' = ' all those
whom '. quos is from the indefinite pronoun **quis,** commonly found in the sense of ' any ' or ' some ' after **si,** and
also after **nisi, num, ne.**

l. 421. **insidiis,** ' by our stratagem '.

tota urbe, local abl. without preposition, which is usually
omitted, even in prose, when the place-phrase includes
totus : ' all over the city '.

l. 422. **mentita,** ' lying ', perf. partic. of a deponent vb.,
used, as so often, in present sense.

l. 423. **ora,** ' speech ', *lit.,* ' mouths '.

l. 425. **dextra,** abl., as the scansion shows.

divae, i.e. Pallas (Minerva).

ad, ' at ', a fairly common use of the preposition.

l. 426. **et,** ' too '.

iustissimus, ' wholly just (man) '.

l. 427. **aequi,** gen. sg. neut. of the adj. used as a noun :
' the right '. **aequi** is objective genitive.

l. 428. **dis aliter visum,** ' the gods willed otherwise ', *lit.,*
' to the gods it seemed good otherwise ', i.e. they decided
that even so noble a man should fall.

l. 429. **a sociis,** i.e. by fellow Trojans, hurling spears from
the roof of Minerva's temple. See l. 410.

Panthu, vocative.

l. 430. **labentem,** ' falling ' =' in thy fall '.

infula. The ' head-band ', entwined with the **vittae** or ' fillets ' (l. 221), which was the mark of a priest.

l. 431. **cineres et flamma,** vocatives : ' O, ashes of Troy, o funeral pyre (*lit.*, last flame) of my people '.

l. 432. **testor,** ' I call (you) to witness ', introducing acc. and infin. (**me**) **vitavisse.**

l. 433. **vices Danaum,** ' exchange (of blows) with the Greeks '.

et si fata, etc., ' and if it had been fated ' (*lit.*, ' if the fates had been ') that I should fall, I earned (that fate) by my deeds ' (**manu**).

l. 435. **aevo,** with **gravior,** is abl. of cause. **vulnere,** l. 436, is similar.

l. 436. **gravior,** supply **erat,** ' was too burdened '.

Ulixi, ' of ', i.e. ' dealt by Ulysses ' : subjective genitive.

l. 437. **vocati,** sc. **sumus.**

l. 438. **pugnam,** object of **cernimus,** l. 441.

ceu . . . forent, ' as if there were '.

l. 439. **forent = essent,** ' there were '.

l. 441. **acta,** ' driven (forward) ', i.e. ' advancing '.

testudine. The **testudo** or ' tortoise ', was the screen of interlocking shields held over their heads by soldiers moving to the assault of a walled position.

l. 442. **parietibus.** The first *i* is consonantal, and the word is scanned as a quadrisyllable.

postis, ' doors ' (synecdoche). **sub,** not ' under ', but ' close to '.

l. 443. **gradibus,** ' up the rungs '.

ad, ' in the way of '.

l. 444. **protecti,** passive participle used as an alternative for active + acc. of reflexive pron., ' protecting themselves '.

l. 445. **contra,** adverb.

ll. 445, 446. **tecta culmina,** ' covered roof ', i.e. ' roof-covering '.

The sense is that the Trojans on the roof wrench loose the roof tiles to serve as missiles against the mounting enemy.

l. 446. **quando,** ' since '. The word only means ' when ' in questions.

ultima, sc. **adesse,** ' that the end is near '.

l. 447. **extrema in morte,** ' at the point of death '. Cf. **extremo in litore,** ' at the water's edge '.

l. 448. **decŏra,** ' graceful creations ', abstract for concrete.

l. 449. **alii,** i.e. other Trojans in addition to those fighting on the roof of the palace.

mucronibus, ' swords ' (synecdoche).

imas, ' below '; literally an adjective, ' lowest '.

l. 451. **instaurati,** sc. **sunt.**

succurrere and the two following infinitives depend, rather unusually, on **instaurati sunt :** ' our courage is renewed to . . . '.

l. 452. **vim** would be **vires** in prose.

l. 453. **limen,** ' door ', **fores,** ' entrance '.

caecae. caecus, properly ' blind ', ' unseeing ', often, as here, is used to mean ' unseen ', ' hidden '.

ll. 453, 454. **pervius usus tectorum inter se Priami,** ' a well-used passage from wing to wing of Priam's palace '. This is a very Vergilian phrase, practically defying literal translation. The essence of it is that Vergil expresses the noun ' passage ' by the adjective **pervius,** and the adjective ' well-used ' by the noun **usus.**

l. 454. **postes,** ' door ', as often—synecdoche.

relicti, ' secluded '.

a tergo, ' *in* rear '. Cf. **a fronte, a dextra,** etc. where the preposition has the same meaning.

ll. 455, 456. **se . . . ferre,** ' to betake herself ', not uncommon Latin for ' go '.

l. 456. **saepius.** No more than **saepe**

Andromache, wife of Priam's eldest son, Hector.

l. 457. **avo,** poetic for **ad avum. avus** = Priam.

Astyanacta, acc. sg., Greek 3rd declension. **Astyanax,** her son and Hector's.

l. 460. **Turrim,** object of three verbs, (i) the participle **adgressi,** (ii) **convellimus,** (iii) **impulimus.**

in praecipiti, 'at the edge'. **praecipiti** is abl. sg. neut., and the literal translation is ' at the sheer (place) '.

summis tectis, abl. of place whence without preposition.

sub, ' up to '.

l. 462. **solitae,** sc. **sunt.** This verb has three subjects, **Troia, naves, castra.**

l. 463. **adgressi.** Best render as finite verb: ' we attacked '.

ferro, ' with iron ', i.e. ' with axes '.

circum, adv., ' all round '.

qua, adv., ' where '.

l. 464. **dabant,** ' revealed '.

l. 465. **sedibus,** ' position '.

ll. 460-465. The translation of these somewhat difficult lines is: ' A tower, standing at the edge, and rising **(eductam)** from the roof top starwards, whence all Troy was wont to be seen, and the ships of the Greeks, and the Grecian camp, we attacked with axes all round, where the topmost storey revealed weak joints, wrenched it from its high position, and gave it a thrust'.

l. 466. **agmina,** ' swarms '.

l. 469. **primo in limine.** Perhaps the ' first door ' will be the ' outermost door '.

l. 470. **telis et luce aena,** *lit.,* ' with weapons and bronze light ', i.e. ' with weapons of flashing bronze '. The expression involves two figures common in Vergil: (i) hendiadys, by which **telis** and **luce aena** are put in parallel construction in the same case, instead of the second part being in the genitive, descriptive of the first ; (ii) in the phrase **luce aena,** the more important idea ' bronze ' is expressed by an adjective, the accessory notion, 'light-reflecting ', by a noun. For other instances of a similar kind cf. l. 116 (hendiadys) and l. 453, **pervius usus.**

l. 471. qualis, ' even as '.

in lucem is out of place. It belongs with **convolvit,** l. 474, and should be left till that verb is reached.

mala, ' rank ' or ' noxious ', the notion being that snake's venom must be produced by the unwholesome nature of the creature's food.

l. 472. Final -a occurs three times in this line. Determine the quantities by scansion.

l. 474. **terga,** ' length ', *lit.,* ' back '.

l. 475. **et linguis,** etc., ' and from his mouth flickers the forked tongue '. This is the meaning, but the literal rendering is ' flickers *from* his mouth *with* ', etc.

l. 476. **Una,** adv. Similarly in l. 477.

Achillis, gen.

l. 477. **Scyria.** Scyros is an island in the Aegean.

l. 478. **flammas,** ' fire-brands '.

l. 479. Scan, to determine the quantity of the final a in correpta and **dura.**

l. 480. **limina** = **portas** (synecdoche).

l. 481. See note on l. 479.

trabe, ' a panel '.

l. 482. **dedit,** ' has made '.

lato ore, ' with wide mouth ', i.e. ' gaping '.

l. 485. **vident,** ' they see '—' they ' being those within.

primo, ' very '.

l. 487. **miscetur.** Vergil frequently uses the verb misceo to suggest *confusion.* Translate ' *rings* with *confused* cries of grief and a turmoil of despair '.

l. 489. **tectis,** local ablative, ' about the halls '.

l. 490. **postis**, ' pillars ', not the ' door-posts ' of ll. 480 and 493.

l. 491. **vi patria**, ' with all the violence of his father '.

Pyrrhus, or **Neoptolemus**, was the son of Achilles.

l. 492. **sufferre**, ' to withstand (him) '.

ariete crebro, abl. of cause, ' under the incessant blows of the battering ram '.

l. 493. In all this description of the forcing of an entry by Pyrrhus, there are signs that Vergil did not very clearly imagine the scene. After four lines (479-482) describing how Pyrrhus breaks the hinges from the door-posts, and then proceeds, it might seem unnecessarily, to hew out a breach in the solid oak of a door panel, we read in l. 493 of the use of a battering ram, surely now supei fluous, and finally of the falling of the door-posts, parted from the hinges. But we have to remember that Vergil himself was so conscious of the imperfections of the *Aeneid* that he gave instructions on his death-bed for the whole poem to be destroyed. Plainly he himself looked on the work we have as a mere first draft.

l. 495. **immissi**, *lit.*, ' sent in (by themselves)', i.e. ' charging in '. Cf. the use of **feror** for ' I rush ', in l. 498 and elsewhere.

milite, ' with soldiery ', concrete for collective.

l. 496. **non sic**, ' not so ', i.e. ' less violently '.

aggeribus, ' banks '.

cum, ' when '.

l. 497. **exiit**, ' has overflowed '.

molis = **aggeres** of l. 496, probably.

l. 498. **furens cumulo**, ' raging with its crest ', i.e. ' in a raging, foam-crested wave '.

l. 499. **trahit**, ' sweeps '.

l. 501. **centumque nurus**. As Hecuba had fifty sons and fifty daughters, the **centum** is made up of the latter and the wives of her sons.

per, ' among '.

l. 502. **quos . . . ignis.** Take **ignis** before **quos . . . sacra-verat.**

l. 504. **barbarico auro spoliisque,** probably hendiadys, ' with the golden spoils of foreign foes '. I.e. the doors of the bridal chambers had been decorated with golden trophies taken in war.

l. 505. **qua,** adv.

l. 506. **et,** ' too '.

fuerint, subjunctive in indirect question.

requiras. Forsitan is regularly used with the subjunctive.

l. 507. **uti** = **ut,** ' when '. In this meaning, and with the meaning of ' as ', **ut** is followed by the indicative.

l. 508. **medium.** Vergil's avoidance of the obvious—we should expect, and must translate, **mediis**—is illustrated here.

l. 509. **senior** amounts here to no more than **senex.**

l. 510. **circumdat** is here constructed with an acc., **arma,** and a dative, **umeris.**

aevo, abl. of cause, with **trementibus.**

l. 511. **cingitur.** Good example of the middle use of the passive voice, i.e. = active + dat. of reflexive pronoun, ' girds on himself '. Cf. note on l. 218.

fertur, ' moves '. Cf. l. 498.

densos in hostis, ' into the thick of the foe '.

moriturus probably indicates destiny rather than intention : ' doomed to die '.

l. 512. **nudo sub aetheris axe.** Vergil imagines the palace of Priam as a typical Roman house, built round a quadrangle open to the sky.

l. 515. **nequiquam** goes with **sedebant,** l. 517. ' In vain ', because the altar did not give them the sanctuary they expected.

circum governs **altaria,** which is pl. for sg.

l. 516. **praecipites,** ' (driven) headlong '.

l. 517. Translate **condensae,** ' huddled together ', and **amplexae** at the end of the sentence.

l. 518. **sumptis,** abl. abs., ' after he had taken up '.

l. 519. **ut vidit.** See note on l. 507. The subject of **vidit** is Hecuba.

mens, ' purpose '.

l. 520. **cingi = cingere te,** a not uncommon use of the passive voice.

l. 521. **istis,** ' such as you '. Remember that **iste** is a demonstrative of the 2nd person, as **hic** is of the 1st, and **is, ille,** of the 3rd.

l. 522. **non,** ' no, not even '.

adforet = adesset. The imperfect subjunctive has the usual meaning of this tense in conditional sentences— supposition contrary to actual fact in present time : ' were here '.

l. 523. **huc,** i.e. to a place at the altar, beside herself.

tandem often accompanies an imperative or interrogative, with the meaning, ' pray '.

l. 524. **moriere.** Parse carefully.

simul, i.e. **nobiscum.**

ore is redundant in English.

l. 526. **Pyrrhi,** subjective genitive, ' wrought by P.'.

l. 527. **porticibus,** local abl., ' down . . . '.

l. 529. **infesto vulnere,** *lit.,* ' with threatening wound ', Vergilian for ' with weapon poised to strike '.

l. 530. **hasta,** abl.

l. 531. **evasit.** See note on **uti vidit,** l. 507.

l. 533. **hic,** temporal adv., ' then '.

in media morte tenetur, ' is held in the very grip of death '.

l. 534. **voci iraeque,** hendiadys, ' voice and anger ' being equal to ' angry words '.

l. 535. **pro,** ' in return for '.

ausis, ' daring ', almost ' sacrilege ' here.

l. 536. qua, ' any ', nom. sg. fem. of qui, indefinite adj.

quae is to be rendered ' such as ', or ' to ', the subjunctive
curet being either generic, a variety of the consecutive, or
final (purpose).

l. 537. persolvant, optative subjunctive, i.e. expressing a
wish or hope : ' may the gods pay '.

l. 538. qui. The antecedent is tibi, l. 535 : ' to you
who . . . '.

coram, adv., ' in my presence '.

l. 539. foedasti = foedavisti.

vultus, acc. pl., ' sight '.

l. 540. satum (esse) quo te mentiris, ' from whom you
falsely-say (mentiris) that you are sprung '.

l. 541. talis in hoste fuit, *lit.*, ' was not such in (the case
of) his foe ', i.e. ' did not so behave towards . . . '.

l. 543. Hectoreum = Hectoris.

l. 544. senior. See note on this word, l. 509.

ictu, properly ' blow ' : render here ' force '.

l. 545. repulsum, sc. est, ' was parried '.

l. 546. summo umbone, ' from the edge of the boss '.
Apparently Priam's spear pierced the leather outer covering
of the shield but was stopped by the metal underneath.

l. 547. Pyrrhus, supply dixit.

nuntius, ' (as) a messenger ', i.e. ' with the news '.

l. 549. degeneremque Neoptolemum : supply esse.

memento, 2nd sg. imperative of memini, as is morere,
l. 550, of morior.

l. 550. trementem and lapsantem, l. 551, agree with eum
(= Priamum) understood.

l. 553. lateri, poetic for in latus.

capulo, governed by the preposition tenus.

haec, sc. erat.

l. 554. **fatorum,** ' destiny '.

l. 555. **illum sorte tulit,** ' befel him by the lottery (of fate) '.

videntem, and **superbum,** l. 556, agree with **illum,** l. 554.

l. 556. **tot populis superbum,** *lit.,* ' proud with ', i.e. ' proud overlord of so many peoples '.

l. 560. **subiit,** ' rose (before me) '.

genitoris, i.e. Anchises.

l. 561. **ut vidi.** See note on **uti vidit,** l. 507.

l. 562. **Creusa,** wife of Aeneas ; Iulus, l. 563, his son.

l. 564. **copia,** ' force ', i.e. of men.

l. 565. **Deseruere,** sc. **me.**

saltu misere (misere for **miserunt),** ' sent with a leap ', i.e. ' hurled '.

l. 566. **aegra dedere,** ' yielded them, overcome '.

l. 567. **adeo,** sometimes inserted to emphasise such words as **iam,** need not be translated.

super unus eram—a case of tmesis, or separation. The verb is **supereram.**

unus, ' alone '.

Vestae. Vergil makes the temples of Troy include one to the Roman goddess of fire. This squares with his purpose of dignifying the history of Rome by linking it up with the great Homeric legend.

l. 568. **servantem,** *lit.,* ' guarding '. No more than ' close to '.

l. 569. **Tyndarida.** ' The daughter of Tyndareus ' is Helen, cause of the Trojan War, and as such particularly hateful to Aeneas.

l. 570. **erranti** and **ferenti** agree with **mihi** understood.

oculos, ' gaze '.

l. 571. The line illustrates a common idiom of Latin by which participles, e.g. **eversa,** and adjectives of similar type, e.g. **infestos,** express what would in English be abstract nouns. Thus ' fearing **(praemetuens,** l. 573) the

Trojans hostile on account of Troy overthrown ' = ' fearing
the *hostility* of the T., on account of Troy's *overthrow* '.

l. 572. **coniugis,** i.e. Menelaus, from whom Paris, son of
Priam, had abducted her, not against her will.'

l. 573. **communis,** translate ' aliᴸᴄ '.

Erinys, ' Fury '. There were three Furies (**Erinyes**) in
Greek mythology. They were goddesses of vengeance.
Aeneas compares Helen, as the instrument of evil fate to
both Greece and Troy, with one of these.

l. 574. **aris,** local abl., ' at . . . '. Notice again how Vergil
is vague in his picturisation of the scene. Helen is ' haunt-
ing the doorway ', ' skulking in a place apart ', and ' sitting
at the altar '; the three expressions, while not necessarily
exclusive of one another, certainly suggest that Vergil had
no clear image in his own mind.

l. 574. **invisa,** ' hateful (creature) '.

l. 575. **animo,** ' in my breast '.

subit, as in l. 562, ' there rises in me '.

ira, ' a passion ', with **ulcisci** and **sumere,** in a rather un-
Latin way, explaining it.

l. 576. **sceleratas,** plainly not ' guilty ' here, but ' of
guilt '.

l. 577. **Spartam,** the city of Helen's husband, Menelaus.
incolumis, ' unscathed '.

l. 578. **parto,** from **pario,** ' gain ', ' win '.

regina, ' (as) a queen '. Simple apposition is often employed in Latin where we use ' as '.

l. 579. **coniugium,** *lit.,* ' marriage ', but used for ' husband '. This is a case of an abstract noun being used
instead of a kindred concrete noun, and is not uncommon in
Latin.

l. 580. **comitata.** The perf. participle of the deponent
verb **comitor** is here used in a *passive* sense.

l. 581. **occiderit,** fut. perf., likewise **arserit** and **sudarit**
(=**sudaverit**). **igni,** an old form of the ablative.

l. 582. sudarit sanguine, ' shall have sweated with blood ', or perhaps ' steamed with the warm blood outpoured '.

l. 583. nomen, ' glory '.

l. 584. feminea in poena. The adjective is equal to an objective genitive **feminae** : ' in taking vengeance on a woman '.

victoria, ' (such a) victory '.

l. 585. exstinxisse depends, in a rather strained construction, upon **laudabor.** Translate ' for having blotted out ', and treat **sumpsisse** similarly.

nefas, ' impious creature ', acc. of an indeclinable noun. Helen is meant.

l. 586. explesse = explevisse.

iuvabit, ' it will please '. The ' it ' is anticipatory, the real subjects being the two perfect infinitives, and the object **me,** understood.

l. 587. flammae, ' with fire '. The genitive is often found after verbs denoting filling and emptying.

l. 588. ferebar, ' and was rushing (on) '.

l. 589. videndam, *lit.,* ' to be seen ', i.e. ' to my sight '.

l. 590. obtulit has subject **parens** (l. 591), object **se. Cum** takes the indicative in such cases as this, where the statement it introduces, while syntactically dependent, is in sense the principal clause. Such clauses are called ' inverse cum ' clauses. For another example study : ' I was just going out when the doctor arrived '—**iam exiturus eram, cum medicus advenit.**

et pura ... refulsit. Venus, (**alma parens**), illuminated by a supernatural radiance, is visible in the surrounding darkness.

l. 591. confessa deam. *Se* and *esse* are to be supplied : ' manifesting herself as a goddess '.

qualisque ... solet. *Lit.* ' (and of such a kind and of such a size) as she is wont ... '. **Talis** and **tanta,** omitted as they often are before their appropriate relatives, must be understood. Translate : ' in such form and stature as ... '.

Usually the gods assumed mortal shape in their appear-

ances to men. Aeneas, son of Venus by Anchises, receives
the special honour of an apparition in divine form.

l. 592. **caelicolis,** dat. of the agent.

prehensum continuit = prehendit et continuit. A participle is the usual way of expressing the first of two verbs
predicated of a single subject. Cf. **nuntium captum inter-
fecerunt,** normal Latin for ' they caught and killed the
messenger '.

l. 594. **tantus = magnus.**

l. 595. **quid.** This is an example of a use of the accusative
case called variously cognate, internal or adverbial. Verbs
such as **furo,** ' am mad ', which obviously cannot take direct
objects, can yet in Latin have their meaning limited by an
accusative. As nearly as we can render it the sense here is,
' What (madness) are you mad with? '—i.e. ' What madness
is this of thine? '

nostri, objective genitive depending on **cura :** ' regard
for me '. **nostri** is for **mei,** as often, but particularly appropriate here, since the speaker is a goddess.

l. 597. **liqueris, superet :** subjunctives in indirect questions.

-ne is for **num,** ' whether '.

l. 598. **quos** is governed by **circum.**

l. 599. **acies,** ' hosts '.

l. 600. **tulerint, hauserit :** the perfect subjunctive is a
possible alternative to the present in conditional sentences :
' would destroy them ', etc.

l. 602. **culpatusve.** We should expect **culpandus :** ' nor
is P. to be blamed '.

l. 603. **opes,** ' power '.

l. 604. **omnem** agrees with **nubem,** l. 606, which is the
antecedent of **quae.**

obducta tuenti, *lit.,* ' drawn before (thee) gazing ', i.e.
' spread before thine eyes '.

l. 605. **umida,** either nom. sg. fem., in which case best
rendered by an adverb ' dankly ', or acc. pl. neut., cognate

acc. (see note on l. 595). In the latter case, taken closely with **caligat**, it will mean : ' spreads a dank gloom '.

l. 606. **qua,** ' any ', acc. pl. neut. of indefinite adjective **qui.**

l. 607. **ne time, neu recusa.** These, expressing negative commands, would be perfect subjunctives in prose.

l. 608. **hic,** adv.

moles, ' masonry '.

l. 610. **emota,** ' loosened '.

l. 612. **Scaeas portas.** ' The Scaean Gate ' was one of the gates of Troy.

l. 613. **prima,** ' first ', i.e. ' in the van ' of Troy's enemies.

socium, adjective, ' confederate ', i.e. consisting of Greeks, whose purpose of destruction Juno shares.

l. 616. **Gorgone saeva.** Pallas wore on her shield the head of the Gorgon, Medusa, severed by Perseus : ' and with the head of the frightful Gorgon '.

l. 617. **Ipse pater,** i.e. Jupiter.

in, ' against '.

l. 618. **arma,** ' forces '.

l. 619. **eripe fugam,** ' snatch thy flight ', i.e. ' fly instantly '.

l. 620. **nusquam abero,** ' I shall be absent nowhere ', i.e. ' I shall be with you everywhere '.

l. 621. **dixerat,** ' she had spoken ' = ' she had done ', or ' she ceased '.

l. 623. **numina,** ' presences '.

l. 624. **visum,** sc. **est.**

l. 625. **ex imo,** ' from the bottom ', i.e. ' from her foundations '. The walls of Troy, which a king of that city contracted with Neptune to build, are now being destroyed by the god, cheated by the king of his agreed reward.

l. 626. **veluti cum,** introducing a simile, as before, l. 379.

l. 627. **ferro,** probably ' with iron (wedge) '.

crebris bipennibus. 'with frequent axes', i.e. 'with blow upon blow of the axe'.

instant, 'strive', with the infin. eruere dependent on it.

l. 628. minatur, 'threatens', i.e. to fall, and so 'totters'.

l. 629. comam, acc. of respect, with tremefacta.

l. 630. supremum congemuit, 'it has groaned its last'. For the acc. supremum see note on quid, l. 595.

l. 631. traxit ruinam. For the same phrase see l. 465. The sense is 'has crashed'.

iugis. Take this with avulsa, as an abl. of separation.

l. 632. ducente deo, abl. abs., 'the divinity leading', i.e· 'led by the divinity'.

flammam is governed by inter.

l. 633. expedior = expedio me, 'I extricate myself', i.e. 'I make my way'. This use of the passive, as an equivalent for active + reflexive pronoun, has been met before.

dant locum, 'give ground', i.e., at the bidding of Venus.

l. 634. perventum sc. est, lit., 'it was come', a common Latin variation for the active used personally, perveni. The construction is called the Impersonal Passive. Cf. pugnatur for pugnant, '(men) fight'.

l. 636. primum, 'first', i.e. 'above all'. Perhaps Vergil's reason for picturing Aeneas as thinking first of Anchises rather than of wife or son is to be found in the poet's own life. Vergil had a particular devotion to his own father and was himself unmarried.

l. 637. excisa Troia, abl. abs., 'now that T. . . . .'.

l. 638. quibus integer aevi sanguis, 'to whom the blood is untouched by time', i.e. 'whose blood the years have not thinned'. The genitive aevi, expressing the instrument, is unusual. Sidgwick quotes a parallel from Ovid, mens interrita leti, 'a spirit undaunted by death'.

l. 639. robore, 'vigour'.

l. 641. voluissent, servassent have the usual meaning of

pluperfect subjunctives in conditional sentences : ' had wished . . . would have saved '.

l. 642. **satis superque vidimus,** ' (it is) enough and more (that) I have seen '.

l. 644. **sic positum,** ' thus placed ', i.e. ' as thus it lies '.

adfati discedite, ' bid farewell to . . . and go '. For the use of the participle see note on **prehensum continuit,** l. 592.

l. 646. From the fact that the ancients attached great importance to the rite of burial, the depth of Anchises' despair can be gauged.

l. 647. **invisus** sc. **sum.** The present tense, when used with **iam pridem, iam diu, iamdudum** is equal to an English perfect : ' this long while I *have been* . . . '.

l. 648. **pater, rex,** i.e. Jupiter, who punished Anchises, a mortal, for boasting of his conquest of the goddess Venus.

l. 650. **memorans. Memoro** does *not* mean ' remember '.

fixus, i.e. in his resolve.

l. 651. **nos** (=**ego**), **coniunx, Ascanius, domus,** are all subjects of some such verb as **oravimus** understood, on which the indirect petition opened by **ne** depends.

contra, adv.

effusi lacrimis, ' outpoured in tears ', Vergilian for ' bursting into tears '.

l. 652. **vertere,** ' to overthrow ', ' wreck '.

incumbere, ' to lean upon ', i.e. ' add his weight to '.

l. 654. **incepto et sedibus in isdem,** ' in the same purpose and the same seat '. Such a coupling of two nouns of different classes (abstract and concrete) is called a zeugma. It was reckoned an ornament in Latin poetry, but English instances of this figure are usually facetious : e.g. ' he took his leave and the wrong umbrella '.

l. 655. **feror.** Probably a true passive here, ' I am prompted '.

in arma, ' to (take up) arms '.

miserrimus, ' in my deep wretchedness '.

l. 656. **dabatur,** ' was given ', i.e. ' was left '.

l. 657. **mene** = me + ne. The order for translation is **sperastine me posse,** etc.

efferre pedem, ' to carry out one's foot ', is ' to depart '.

te, abl., with **relicto.**

l. 658. **ore** =' lips ', as often.

l. 659. The order is **si placet superis nihil relinqui.**

nihil relinqui, acc. and infin., ' that nothing should be left '.

l. 661. **te** is object of **addere.** A second **te** is wanted, object of **iuvat,** ' it is your pleasure '.

-que . . . -que, ' both ', ' and '.

isti, dat., (with **leto**) as usual, =' that of yours ', i.e. ' which you have chosen '.

l. 662. **multo de sanguine,** *lit.,* ' from the much blood ', i.e. ' from spilling the blood '.

l. 663. **qui** must be taken first in the line.

l. 664. **hoc erat quod . . . ,** ' was it for this that . . . '. The case of **hoc** is open to doubt—possibly it is an abl. of cause, ' on this account '.

parens, i.e. Venus.

l. 665. **eripis.** Best turned by a past tense in English.

l. 667. **alterum in alterius,** ' each in the other's '.

cernam, final, ' that I should see '.

l. 668. **lux,** ' dawn '.

l. 669. **revisam,** instead of the usual **me revisere.**

l. 671. **hinc,** adv. of time.

accingor = me accingo. Cf. **expedior** and note, l. 633.

l. 672. **aptans,** ' fitting it into place '.

me ferebam, ' was rushing '. **ferebar** would have had the same sense.

l. 675. **periturus,** ' to your death ', *lit.,* ' about to perish '.

et, ' too '.

in omnia, ' to face all your perils '.

l. 676. **expertus,** ' having tried ', i.e. ' from your experience '.

sumptis. Translate by adjectival clause.

l. 677. **tutare.** Parse carefully.

l. 678. **et coniunx.** The order is **et (ego) quondam dicta coniunx tua.**

relinquor. Understand from this verb, **relinquitur,** having as subjects **Iulus** and **pater.**

l. 680. **dictu,** supine in -u (really abl. case of a verbal noun) depends on **mirabile,** ' marvellous in the telling ', i.e. ' marvellous to tell '.

oritur, ' there occurs '.

l. 681. **inter** governs both **manus** and **ora.**

l. 682. **visus,** sc. **est.**

l. 683. **apex,** ' point ' or ' tongue, of flame '.

tactu dependent on **innoxia.** Cf. **dictu,** l. 680 and note.

l. 684. **tempora,** ' temples ', not ' time ', here. Note this meaning.

l. 685. **pavidi,** ' in our terror '.

ll. 685, 686. **trepidare, excutere, restinguere** are historic infinitives, i.e. infinitives used instead of historic tenses of the indicative, most commonly the imperfect, as here. **trepidare** is ' quaked ', **excutere,** ' sought to dash out ' (*conative* use of imperfect).

crinem flagrantem, ' the blazing hair ' where, after **excutere,** we should expect ' the fire from the hair '.

l. 686. **sanctos,** because supernatural.

fontibus, no more than **aquā.**

l. 687. **laetus,** adj. for adv.

l. 688. **cum voce,** variation for **et vocem.**

tetendit, ' uplifted '.

l. 690. **hoc tantum,** sc. **precor,** ' I pray '. tantum is the adverb, ' only '.

l. 691. **deinde,** usually ' then '. Here, plainly ' now '.

l. 692. **senior** = **senex** as before.

subitoque. We should say ' when ' rather than ' and ' for the -**que.**

l. 693. **intonuit laevum,** ' it thundered left ', where we must say ' on the left '. **laevum** is another example of the acc. explained in the note on **quid,** l. 595. Thunder on the left was a good omen for Romans.

lapsa. Perfect participles of deponent verbs are often used with present meaning.

l. 694. **facem ducens,** ' leading a torch ' is plainly ' with fiery tail '.

cucurrit, ' sped ' or ' shot '.

l. 696. **claram se condere,** ' bury itself bright ', i.e. ' bury its bright self '.

Idaea silva, abl. of place where without preposition.

l. 697. **tum,** etc. There is a glow left in the sky along the track (**limes**) which the shooting star has followed.

l. 699. **hic,** adv. of time.

victus, ' overborne ', i.e. convinced by the portents of the gods' wish that he should seek to escape.

ad auras is almost redundant, and untranslateable anyway. Say ' up '.

l. 703. **numine,** ' power '.

l. 704. **tibi comes ire,** ' to go (as) companion to you ', i.e. ' to accompany you '.

l. 705. **dixerat.** See note, l. 621.

clarior, adj. for adv.

ignis. Plainly ' the (roar of the) fire '.

l. 706. **aestus,** acc. pl.

l. 707. **age,** often used with another imperative in the same way as English ' come '.

imponere, 2 sg. imperative pass. Here again the passive = active + reflexive, **te impone.**

l. 708. **subibo,** ' will support (you) '.

nec me labor, etc.   Anchises is shrunken with age and deformity.

l. 709. **quo cumque,** a single word separated for metrical convenience.   This is called tmesis.

cadent, ' shall turn out '.

l. 710. **ambobus,** sc. **nobis.**

l. 711. **sit, servet,** jussive subjunctives, ' let . . . '.   **sit comes,** ' accompany '.   **servare** here is ' follow in '.

l. 713. **est urbe egressis tumulus,** ' there is (to you) having gone out from the city a mound ', i.e. ' leaving the city you will come upon . . . '.

l. 714. **iuxta,** adv.

l. 716. **ex diverso,** ' from different directions '.

l. 717. **sacra,** ' the sacred things ' are presumably the altar vessels and utensils.

penatis, small statues of the family gods.

l. 718. **digressum,** best rendered by a relative clause, ' who have . . . ,' agrees with **me.**

l. 719. **me attrectare,** acc. infin., ' that I should touch them ', dependent on **nefas (est),** ' it is wrong '.

l. 719. **vivo,** ' living ', i.e. ' flowing ', not stagnant.

l. 721. **subiecta,** ' bowed '.

l. 722. **super,** adv.

fulvique.   Drop the -que and take **pelle** in apposition with **veste,** ' with a covering, the skin . . . '.

insternor, ' I overlay '.   Middle use of passive voice, here with **umeros** and **colla** as direct objects.   See note, l. 218.

l. 723. **succedo,** ' undergo ', i.e. ' submit myself to '.

dextrae se implicuit, ' entwined himself in (my) right hand ', i.e. ' clasped my right hand '.

l. 725. **pone,** adv.

ferimur.   Once again passive for active + reflexive : ' we take ourselves ', ' we go '.

opaca locorum, variation for **opacos locos**, like **lapsus rotarum**, l. 235.

me, object of **terrent**, l. 728.

l. 726. **movebant**, ' troubled '.

l. 727. **adverso ex agmine**, ' in hostile array '. Place whence prepositions are often found in Latin where English uses place where prepositions. For a common instance cf. **a tergo**, ' in the rear '.

l. 728. **omnes aurae**, ' every gust of wind '.

l. 729. **suspensum**, ' anxious (as I am) '.

l. 730. **videbar**, ' seemed ', common meaning of the passive of **video**.

l. 731. **evasisse**, ' to have traversed '.

creber goes in grammar with **sonitus**, in sense with **pedum**: ' the sound of many feet '.

l. 732. **visus sc. est**, indicative in an inverse cum clause. Cf. note, l. 590.

adesse, ' to come '.

l. 735. **hic**, adverb of time.

mihi. The dative is frequently used to translate ' from ' after compound verbs meaning ' to take away '.

nescio quod, often written as one word, ' I know not what ', i.e. ' some '. Translate with **numen**.

male amicum, ' unfriendly ', **male** having the same negative force as in **male fida**, l. 23.

l. 736. **avia**, neut. pl. of the adj. used as a noun.

cursu, abl. of manner, ' at a run '.

misero qualifies **mihi** understood. For the dative see note on **mihi**, l. 735.

l. 738. **fatone** =**fato** + **ne**, the **-ne** asking a direct question.

l. 739. **via**—**e via** in prose.

l. 740. **incertum sc. est**.

post, adv.

l. 741. **prius** separated as often from its **quam**. **priusquam** is ' before ', or ' until '.

amissam, ' my lost one '.

l. 742. **tumulum, sedem,** accusatives of the goal of motion without preposition : ' to the mound ', etc.

l. 743. **una,** ' alone '.

l. 744. **fefellit,** ' disappointed ', ' failed to meet '.

l. 745. **amens,** adj. for adv.

l. 748. **curva valle,** abl. of place where.

recondo. The object is **eos** understood.

l. 749. **cingor** = me cingo.

l. 750. **stat,** *lit.,* ' it stands ', ' it is fixed ', i.e. ' I am resolved '.

renovare, ' to renew ', i.e. ' to face anew '.

l. 753. **gressum extuleram,** ' I had carried out my step ', i.e. ' I had come out '.

l. 754. **observata sequor,** ' I search out and follow '. For the use of the participle cf. **prehensum continuit,** l. 592, and note.

lumine = oculo, as often in poetry.

l. 755. **animos,** pl. for sg.

l. 756. **si forte,** ' if haply ', i.e. ' in case '.

pedem tulisset = iisset simply. Supply **eo,** ' thither '. The subjunctive **tulisset** is due to oratio obliqua. Aeneas is reporting his own thoughts.

l. 759. **ad auras,** ' skywards '.

l. 761. **porticibus, asylo,** both abls. of place where.

l. 763. **Troia,** adjective.

l. 765. **auro solidi,** ' solid with gold ', Vergilian for ' of solid gold '.

l. 766. **pueri,** etc. These, intended to be sold as slaves, would form a valuable part of the booty.

l. 768. **ausus,** with present meaning, which is commonly

allowed in the case of perfect participles of deponent and semi-deponent verbs.

quin etiam, ' nay, even '.

l. 769. **maestus,** adj. for adv.

Creüsam, ' (the name of) Creusa '.

l. 771. **quaerenti** and **furenti** agree with **mihi,** l. 773. Translate by adverbial clauses, ' as I searched ', etc.

tectis, local abl., ' among the buildings '. **tectum,** properly ' roof ', is here, as often, used by synecdoche for ' building ', ' house '.

ll. 772, 773. Drop both **atque** and **et** in translation. This is another case where simple apposition is preferred in English.

simulacrum, umbra, imago are nearly the same thing. All are words for the apparition of Creusa which confronts Aeneas.

l. 773. **visa** sc. **est,** ' appeared '.

nota, abl. of comparison after **maior,** *lit.,* ' than the known (woman)', i.e. ' than the woman I had known '.

l. 774. **steterunt,** with the middle syllable, irregularıy, short.

l. 775. **adfari, demere,** historic infinitives. See note on l. 685. The subject is **Creüsa.**

l. 776. **quid iuvat** sc. **te,** ' what does it help you? ' i.e. ' what use is it? '

tantum, acc. of extent, ' so deeply ', is best taken as modifying **indulgere.**

l. 777. **haec.** ' These things ', of course, are the capture and destruction of Troy.

l. 778. **te portare,** acc. and infin., ' that you should carry ', subject to (est) **fas,** ' it is right '.

comitem, ' (as) companion '.

l. 779. **ille,** ' the great ', not uncommon with such a meaning in Latin prose too.

regnator, Jupiter, of course.

l. 780. **longa,** sc. **sunt. exsilia is pl. for sg.**

aequor arandum est tibi, ' there is for you an expanse to be ploughed ', i.e. ' and you must plough . . . '.

l. 781. **terram Hesperiam,** ' to the land of Italy ', *lit.,* ' the land of the Evening Star ', a name that the Greeks, looking westward, gave to the sister peninsula of Italy. Note (i) acc. of the goal of motion without preposition, for which cf. **tumulum,** l. 742, and (ii) the Latin way of saying ' land of Italy ' ; cf. **urbs Roma,** ' city *of* Rome '.

Lydius. The north bank of the Tiber was Etruscan, and that little-known and non-Italian people was by tradition supposed to originate from Lydia (Asia Minor).

l. 782. **opima virum,** ' rich in men ', the reference being to both quantity and quality of population, no doubt. Vergil, writing by imperial command a patriotic epic, suggests that Rome's greatest treasure is her sons. The genitive **virum** (= **virorum**) is that found after words denoting fulness.

agmine, ' course '.

l. 783. **res laetae,** ' happiness ', *lit.,* ' happy circumstances '. For similar uses of **res,** cf. **res secundae,** ' success ', **res novae,** ' revolution '.

l. 784. **parta** (from **pario**), sc. **sunt,** ' are won '.

l. 785. **non aspiciam.** Creusa assures Aeneas that her destiny is not capture and bondage among the Greeks.

l. 786. **servitum,** ' to be a slave ', the supine in -m (acc. case of a verbal noun), expressing purpose after a verb of motion. It is really exactly parallel in construction to **terram,** l. 781, and the literal rendering is ' nor shall I go to slavery to Greek matrons '.

l. 787. **Dardanis** and **nurus** are in apposition to **ego,** l. 785.

l. 788. **magna genetrix** is Cybele, an Asiatic goddess later worshipped at Rome.

l. 790. **lacrimantem** and **volentem** agree with me understood.

l. 792. **conatus** sc. **sum.**

collo is dative after the compound **circumdare**, which is divided and reversed.

dare, ' to put '.

l. 793. **manus,** acc. pl.

ll. 796, 797. **numerum adfluxisse,** acc. and infin. dependent on **invenio,** ' I discover that . . . '.

l. 798. **exsilio,** dat. of purpose, ' for exile '.

l. 799. **convenere** = **convenerunt.**

l. 800. Something like ' to follow me ' needs to be inserted before commencing the translation of this line.

velim. Perhaps the subjunctive is in imitation, not necessarily conscious, of the Greek construction in indefinite relative clauses. Remember that Vergil, and indeed all the Latin poets, were close students of Greek literature.

pelago, abl. of route, ' over the sea '.

l. 801. **summae,** in grammar with **Idae,** in sense with **iugis,** ' highest peaks '.

l. 802. **obsessa,** ' guarded '.

l. 803. **opis,** ' of aid ' (by me, Aeneas).

98

VERGIL : THE STANDING FIGURES ARE THE MUSES
OF HISTORY (LEFT) AND TRAGEDY.
(From a Roman mosaic found at Sousse, Tunisia, a town
near the site of the ancient Hadrumetum.)

VOCABULARY

N.B.—In the following vocabulary the figures (1), (2), (3), (4), after the verbs, denote the conjugation. No conjugation number is given in the case of -*io* verbs like *capio*.

A

ā *or* ab, *prep.* +*abl.*, from, by.

abdō, didī, ditum (3), hide, conceal ; *of a weapon*, plunge.

abeō, īvī *or* iī, itum, go away, depart.

abiēs, etis, *f.*, pine-tree, fir.

abluō, luī, lūtum (3), wash away, cleanse, purify.

abnegō, āvī, ātum (1), refuse.

abstineō, uī, entum (2), refrain, abstain.

absum, āfuī, to be away from, absent.

ac *or* atque, *conj.*, and.

Acamās, antis, *m.*, one of the Greeks concealed in the wooden horse.

accīdō, cīdī, cīsum (3), cut, hew.

accingō, īnxi, īnctum (3), gird on ; gird, l. 614.

accipiō, ere, ēpī, eptum, receive, take, admit, learn, listen.

accommodō, āvī, ātum (1), adjust to, adapt.

ācer, cris, cre, *adj.*, violent, hasty, fierce.

acernus, a, um, *adj.*, made of maple.

Achāicus, a, um, *adj.*, Greek, Grecian.

Achillēs, is *and* ī, *m.*, son of Peleus, King of Thessaly, and Thetis ; one of the greatest heroes at the siege of Troy.

Achīvī, ōrum, *m.*, Greeks.

aciēs, iēī, *f.*, edge, line of battle, battle.

ad, *prep.* +*acc.*, towards, near to.

addō, didī, ditum (3), add, attach.

adeō, *adv.*, so far, indeed.

adflīgō, īxī, īctum (3), cast down, afflict.

adflō, āvī, ātum (1), blow upon.

adfluō, ūxī (3), flow to, flock up, throng.

adfor, fātus (1 *dep.*), speak to, address.

adglomerō, āvī, ātum (1), crowd together.

adgnōscō, ōvī, itum (3), recognise.

adgredior, ī, gressus, set about, assault.

adhūc, *adv.*, up to this time, still.

aditus, ūs, *m.*, entrance, approach.

admīror, ātus, (1 *dep.*), wonder, be astonished, admire.

adōrō, āvī, ātum (1), speak to, accost, reverence.

adpāreō, ui, ītum (2), appear.
adsentiō, ēnsī, ēnsum (4), approve.
adservō, āvī, ātum (1), guard.
adtrectō, āvī, ātum (1), touch, handle.
adsum, fuī, be present, be at hand.
adversus, a, um, adj., turned towards, opposite, hostile.
adytum, ī, n., shrine, sanctuary.
aedēs, is, f. sing., temple ; plur., abode.
aedificō, āvī, ātum (1), build, construct.
aeger, gra, grum, adj., sick, weary, sad.
Aenēās, ae, m., son of Anchises and Venus, and ancestor of the Romans.
aēnus (ahēnus), a, um, adj., of bronze or copper.
aequaevus, a, um, adj., of like age.
aequō, āvī, ātum (1), make equal, equal.
aequor, oris, n., level surface, sea.
aequus, a, um, adj., equal, just.
aerātus, a, um, covered with bronze.
aes, aeris, n., bronze, copper.
aestus, ūs, m., heat, glow.
aetas, tātis, f., age.
aeternus, a, um, adj., eternal, everlasting.
aether, eris, m., air, sky.
aevum, ī, n., age, season, life.
ager, grī, m., field.
agger, eris, m., mound, rampart.
agitātor, ōris, m., driver, charioteer.

agitō, āvī, ātum (1), drive, pursue, turn over in mind.
āgmen, inis, n., line of march ; multitude, course.
agō, ēgi, āctum (3), do, lead, urge on.
agricola, ae, m., husbandman, farmer.
Aiāx, ācis, m., son of Oileus, king of the Locrians in Greece.
āiō, v. defect., say.
aliquī, qua, quod, pron. indef. adjvī., some, any.
aliquis, quid, pron. indef. substantival, someone, something.
aliter, adv., in another manner, otherwise.
alius, a, ud, adj., another (of many) (aliī . . . aliī, some . . . others).
almus, a, um, adj., gentle, propitious.
altāria, n. plur., altar.
alter, a, um, adj., the other (of two) (alter, the one ; alter, the other).
altus, a, um, adj., high, deep ; altum, n., the sea.
alvus, ī, f., belly.
ambiguus, a, um, adj., doubtful, uncertain.
ambo, ae, o, plur. adj., both.
āmēns, entis, adj., out of one's mind, mad.
amīcus, a, um, adj., loving, friendly.
amīcus, i, m., friend.
āmittō, īsī, issum (3), lose, let go.
amor, ōris, m., love, desire.
amplector, xus (3 dep.), wind around, embrace.

amplus, a, um, *adj.*, large, spacious.

an, *conj.*, whether, or.

Anchīsēs, ae, *m.* (*acc.* ēn), father of Aeneas.

Androgeōs, eī, *m.*, a Greek, killed by Aeneas and his followers on the night that Troy was taken.

Andromachē, ēs, *f.*, wife of Hector.

anguis, is, *c.*, snake, serpent.

angustus, a, um, *adj.*, narrow; *as neut. subs.*, angustum, *n.*, a narrow place, a pass.

anima, ae, *f.*, breath, life.

animus, ī, *m.*, spirit, courage, mind.

annus, ī, *m.*, year.

ante, *adv.* and *prep.*; (1) *adv.* before, previously; (2) *prep.* + *acc.* before, in front of.

antīquus, a, um, *adj.*, old, ancient, former.

aperiō, eruī, ertum (4), open, disclose.

apex, icis, *m.*, point, top.

Apollō, inis, *m.*, sun-god, son of Jupiter, brother of Diana.

appāreō, uī, itum (2), come in sight, be visible, appear.

aptō, āvī, ātum (1), fit, adjust.

apud, *prep.*, among, with, *gov. acc.*

āra, ae, *f.*, altar.

arbor, oris, *f.*, tree.

arceō, uī (*no sup.*) (2), confine, restrain, ward off.

ardeō, ārsī, ārsum (2), be on fire, blaze.

arduus, a, um, *adj.*, high, lofty.

Argīvus, a, um, *adj.*, Argive, Greek.

Argolicus, a, um, *adj.*, Argolic, Greek.

Argos, *n.*, and Argi, -orum, *m. pl.*, capital of Argolis in the Peloponnesus

ariēs, etis, *m.*, ram; *hence* battering-ram.

arma, ōrum, *n. plur.*, arms, weapons; battle.

armentum, ī, *n.*, herd, flock.

armiger, erī, *m.*, armour-bearer.

armipotēns, entis, *adj.*, powerful in arms.

armō, āvī, ātum (1), arm, furnish with weapons.

arō, āvī, ātum (1), plough.

arrigō, ēxī, ēctum (3), lift up, keep straight; arrēctīs auribus, with attentive ears.

ars, tis, *f.*, skill, art, cunning, artifice.

artifex, icis, *c.*, contriver, plotter, inventor.

artus, a, um, *adj.*, close-fitting, tight.

arvum, ī, *n.*, field.

arx, cis, *f.*, citadel.

Ascānius, iī, *m.* (also called Iūlus), son of Aeneas and Creusa.

ascendō, endī, ēnsum (3), go up, mount.

ascēnsus, ūs, *m.*, climbing.

Asia, -ae, *f.*, Asia Minor.

asper, era, erum, *adj.*, rough, fierce, cruel.

aspicio, ere, spēxī, aspectum, look on, behold, see.

ast *or* at, *conj.*, but, yet.

Astyanax, actis, *m.*, son of Hector and Andromache.

asylum, *n.*, sanctuary.

āter, tra, trum, *adj.*, black, dark.

atque, *see* ac.

Atrīdae, ārum, *m.*, sons of Atreus—Agamemnon and Menelaus.

ātrium, ī, *n.*, hall.

attollō (*no perf. or sup.*) (3), lift up, raise, erect.

attrecto = adtrecto.

audeō, ausus sum, (2), venture, dare.

audio, īvī, ītum (4), hear, listen.

augurium, iī, *n.*, augury, omen.

aura, ae, *f.*, air, breeze.

aurātus, a, um, *adj.*, covered with gold, gilt.

aureus, a, um, *adj.*, golden.

auris, is, *f.*, ear.

aurum, ī, *n.*, gold.

Auster, stri, *m.*, south wind.

ausum, -i, *n.*, daring, attempt.

aut, *conj.*, or (aut . . . aut, either . . . or).

autem, *conj.*, but, however.

Automedōn, ontis, *m.*, charioteer of Achilles.

auxilium, iī, *n.*, aid, help.

āvehō, ēxi, ēctum (3), carry away ; *pass.*, sail away.

āvellō, vulsī, vulsum (3), pluck, tear off, *or* from.

āvertō, tī, sum (3), turn away from, alienate.

āvius, a, um, *adj.*, out of the way (as *noun* āvium, iī, *n.*, by-path).

avus, ī, *m.*, grandfather.

axis, is, *m.*, axle-tree; axis of the earth, *hence* the heavens.

B

barba, ae, *f.*, beard.

barbaricus, a, um, *adj.*, barbarian, foreign.

Bēlidēs, ae, *m.*, a descendant of Belus, *i.e.* Palamedes.

bellum, ī, *n.*, war, combat.

bīgae, ārum, *f. plur.*, two-horse chariot.

bipatēns, ntis, *adj.*, with two leaves, double.

bipennis, is, *f.*, two-edged axe.

bis, *adv.*, twice.

bonus, -a, -um, good.

bōs, bovis (*gen. plur.* boum), *c.*, ox *or* cow.

bracchium, iī, *n.*, arm.

breviter, *adv.*, shortly, briefly.

brūma, ae, *f.*, winter.

C

cadō, cecidī, cāsum (3), fall, come to pass.

caecus, a, um, *adj.*, blind, hidden, secret.

caedēs, is, *f.*, slaughter.

caedō, cecīdī, caesum (3), cut down, slay.

caelicola, ae, *c.*, heaven-dweller, deity.

caelum, ī, *n.*, heaven, sky.

caerulus, a, um, *adj.*, azure, seagreen, dark.

Calchās, antis, *m.*, chief of the Greek soothsayers at the siege of Troy.

cālīgō, āvi, ātum (1), to obscure, make dark, spread darkness.

campus, ī, *m.*, plain.

canō, cecinī, cantum (3), sing.

capiō, ere, cēpī, captum, take, lay hold of.

captīvus, a, um, *adj.*, captive, taken as spoil.

capulus, ī, *m.*, hilt of a sword.

caput, itis, *n.*, head.

Capys, yos, *m.*, one of the Trojans who advised the destruction of the wooden horse.

cardō, inis, *m.*, hinge.

careō, uī, itum (2), to be without, *gov. abl.*

carīna, ae, *f.*, keel, *hence* ship.

cārus, a, um, *adj.*, dear, beloved.

Cassandra, ae, *f.*, daughter of Priam and Hecuba, whom Apollo gifted with prophecy, but caused her predictions never to be believed.

cassus, a, um, *adj.*, wanting, deprived of (*abl.*).

castra, ōrum, *n. plur.*, camp.

cāsus, ūs, *m.*, chance, accident, misfortune, peril.

caterva, ae, *f.*, crowd, troop.

catulus, ī, *m.*, cub, whelp.

causa, ae, *f.*, cause, reason.

caverna, ae, *f.*, cavern.

cavō, āvī, ātum (1), to hollow, pierce.

cavus, a, um, *adj.*, hollow.

cēdō, cessī, cessum (3), go away, yield.

celsus, a, um, *adj.*, high.

centum, *adj. indecl.*, a hundred.

Cerēs, eris, *f.*, Ceres, goddess of agriculture.

cernō, crēvī, crētum (3), perceive, discern.

certātim, *adv.*, earnestly, vying with another.

certō, āvī, ātum (1), fight, contend, vie.

certus, a, um, *adj.*, fixed, sure.

cervīx, īcis, *f.*, neck.

cesso, āvī, ātum (1), cease.

cēterus, a, um, *adj.* (rare in *sing.*), the other, the remaining.

ceu, *adv.*, as, just like.

cieō, cīvī, citum (2), rouse, stir up.

cingō, cīnxī, cīnctum (3), gird, surround.

cinis, eris, *m.*, ashes.

circum, *adv.* and *prep.* ; (1) *adv.* around, round about ; (2) *prep.* + *acc.*, around.

circumdō, dedī, datum (1), put around, used with *acc.* and *dat.*, i.e. *acc.* of the thing placed, and *dat.* of the object around which it is placed.

circumfundō, fūdī, fūsum (3), pour round ; *in pass.*, crowd, gather round.

circumspiciō, ere, spēxī, spectum, look around upon.

circumstō, stetī (*no sup.*) (1), stand around.

circumvolō, āvī, ātum (1), fly around.

cīvis, is, *c.*, citizen.

clādēs, is, *f.*, slaughter, disaster.

clāmor, ōris, *m.*, outcry, shouting.

clangor, ōris, *m.*, blare of trumpets.

clārēscō, clāruī (*no sup.*) (3), become distinct.

clārus, a, um, *adj.*, clear, distinct.

classis, is, *f.*, fleet.

claustrum, ī, *n.*, bolt, bar.

clipeus, eī, *m.*, shield.

coeptus, a, um, *perf. part.* of coepī, begun.

cōgnōscō, ōvī, itum (3), become acquainted with, know.

cōgō, coēgī, coāctum (3), drive together, force.

colligō, ēgī, ēctum (3), gather together, collect.

collum, ī, *n.*, neck.

coluber, brī, *m.*, snake.

columba, ae, *f.*, dove.

coma, ae, *f.*, hair, *plur.* ; (*of trees*) leaves.

comāns, antis (*part.* of como), furnished with hair, crested.

comes, itis, *c.*, companion.

comitor, ātus sum (1), accompany, attend.

commendō, āvī, ātum (1), confide, entrust.

commūnis, e, *adj.*, common.

compāgēs, is, *f.*, fastening, joint.

compellō, āvī, ātum (1), address, speak to.

complector, exus (3), embrace, encircle.

compleō, ēvī, ētum (2), fill up.

compositō, *adv.* according to agreement.

comprēndō, ēndī, ēnsum (3), seize.

comprimō, essī, essum (3),check, suppress.

concēdō, cessī, cessum (3), depart, retire.

concidō, cidī (*no sup.*) (3), fall down (*especially in death*).

concilium, ī, *n.*, council, l. 88.

conclāmō, āvī, ātum (1), cry out, shout.

concrētus, a, um, *adj.*, matted together, stiffened.

concurrō, currī (*rarely* cucurrī), cursum (3), run together.

concutiō, ere, cussī, cussum, shake violently.

condēnsus, a, um, *adj.*, very thick, close together.

condō, didī, ditum (3), hide, conceal, put together.

cōnfertus, a, um, *adj.*, in a body, compact.

cōnfīgō, fīxī, fīxum (3), fix together, pierce, transfix.

cōnfiteor, fessus (2), confess, acknowledge.

cōnflīgō, flīxī, flīctum (3), engage, contend.

cōnfundō, fūdī, fūsum (3), throw into confusion.

congemō, gemuī (*no sup.*) (3), heave a deep sigh.

congerō, gessī, gestum (3), heap, pile up.

congredior, ī, gressus, engage, fight, contend.

coniciō, ere, iēcī, iectum, hurl, throw.

coniugium, iī, *n.*, marriage, husband, wife.

coniūnx, iugis, *c.*, husband, wife.

cōnor, ātus sum (1), attempt, endeavour.

cōnsanguinitas, ātis, *f.*, relationship (*by blood*).

cōnscius, a, um, *adj.*, confederate, privy to, conscious of, acquainted with.

cōnsequor, cūtus sum (3), attend, accompany.

cōnserō, uī, tum (3), join ; cōnserere proelium, to come to close fighting.

cōnsīdō, sēdī, sessum (3), settle,
sink down.

cōnsilium, ii, *n.*, counsel, advice,
plan.

cōnsistō, stitī, stitum (3), stand
still.

cōnspectus, ūs, *m.*, gazing at,
sight, view.

cōnsūmō, sūmpsī, sūmptum (3),
to take wholly, spend.

contexō, texuī, textum (3), weave
together, form, construct.

conticēscō, ticuī (*no sup.*) (3),
become silent.

contineō, uī, entum (2), hold
back, restrain.

contingō, tigī, tāctum (3), lay
hold of, seize, touch.

contorqueō, torsī, tortum (2),
hurl violently.

contrā, *adv.* and *prep.* ; (1) *adv.*,
on the other side *or* hand ;
(2) *prep.* + *acc.*, against.

contrārius, a, um, *adj.*, opposite,
contrary.

convellō, vellī, vulsum (3), pluck
off, tear away.

conveniō, vēnī, ventum (4),
come together, meet.

convertō, tī, sum (3), turn,
change.

convolvō, volvī, volūtum (3), roll
together.

cōpia, ae, *f.*, plenty, *plur.* cōpiae,
forces, troops.

cōram, *prep. gov. abl.*, in presence of.

Coroebus, ī, *m.*, an ally of Priam,
suitor of Cassandra.

corpus, oris, *n.*, body.

corripio, ere, ripuī, reptum, lay
hold of, carry off, plunder.

coruscus, a, um, *adj.*, flashing,
glittering.

costa, ae, *f.*, rib.

crātēr, ēris, *m.*, bowl, goblet.

crēber, bra, brum, *adj.*, frequent,
repeated, numerous.

crēdō, didī, ditum (3), put faith
in ; *also with dat.*, believe,
think.

crētus, a, um, *perf. part.* of
crēsco, crēvi, crētum, born,
sprung, descended from.

Creūsa, ae, *f.*, daughter of
Priam, wife of Aeneas.

crīmen, inis, *n.*, charge, accusation, crime.

crīnis, is, *m.*, hair (*of the head*).

crūdēlis, e, *adj.*, cruel, wrathful.

cruentus, a, um, *adj.*, blood-
stained.

culmen, inis, *n.*, height, summit.

culpa, ae, *f.*, fault.

culpātus, a, um, *perf. partic.*
pass. of culpō, blamable.

cum, *conj.* and *prep.* ; (1) *conj.*,
when, since ; (2) *prep.* + *abl.*,
with.

cumulus, ī, *m.*, heap.

cūnctus, a, um, *adj.*, all, the
whole.

cupīdō, inis, *f.*, desire.

cupiō, ere, īvī, *or* iī, ītum, desire,
long for.

cupressus, ī, *f.*, cypress-tree.

cūr, *adv.*, why.

cūra, ae, *f.*, care, attention,
regard for.

cūrō, āvī, ātum (1), care for,
take care of, attend to.

currō, cucurrī, cursum (3), run.

cursus, ūs, *m.*, running, speed.

curvus, a, um, *adj.*, bent, curved.

cuspis, idis, *f.*, point, *hence* spear, lance.

cŭstōs, ōdis, *c.*, guard, keeper.

D

Danaī, ōrum (Danaūm), *m.*, (descendants of Danaus, son of Belus, who founded Argos); the Greeks.

Dardanus, ĭ, *m.*, son of Jupiter, ancestor of the royal house of Troy.

Dardania, ae, *f.*, Troy.

Dardanidae, ārum (Dardanidūm), *m.*, the Trojans.

Dardanis, idis, *f.*, a Trojan woman.

Dardanius, a, um, *adj.*, Trojan.

dē, *prep.* + *abl.*, from, down from.

dea, ae, *f.*, goddess.

dēbeo, uī, itum (2), owe.

decem, *num. adj. indecl.*, ten.

decŏrus, a, um, *adj.*, graceful, elegant.

dēcurrō, currī *or* cucurrī, cursum (3), run down.

decus, oris, *n.*, ornament, honour.

dēdūcō, dūxī, ductum (3), lead away, lead from.

dēfendō, fendī, fēnsum (3), ward off, protect.

dēfēnsor, ōris, *m.*, protector, defender.

dēfatīscor, fessus (3), to be weary, tired out.

dēficiō, ere, fēcī, fectum, fail, cease.

dēgener, eris, *adj.*, degenerate, unworthy of one's race.

deinde, *adv.*, then, in the next place.

Dēiphobus, ī, *m.*, a son of Priam.

dēlābor, lāpsus (3), glide down, slip down.

dēligō, lēgī, lēctum (3), choose out, select.

dēlitēscō, lituī (*no sup.*) (3), hide oneself.

dēlūbrum, brī, *n.*, temple, shrine.

dēmēns, entis, *adj.*, out of one's mind, mad, foolish.

dēmittō, īsī, issum (3), let down, lower, let go.

dēmō, psī, ptum (3), take away, remove.

dēmoror, morātus sum (1), delay, detain.

dēmum, *adv.*, at length.

dēnique, *adv.*, then, at length.

dēnsus, a, um, *adj.*, thick, close.

dēpāscor, pāstus (3), feed upon, devour.

dēpōnō, posuī, positum (3), put down, lay aside.

dēscendo, endī, ēnsum (3), come *or* go down, descend.

dēserō, uī, tum (3), forsake.

dēstinō, āvī, ātum (1), appoint, mark out, destine.

dēsūetus, *perf. partic. pass.* of dēsūescō, disused, laid aside.

dēsum, fuī, be away, be wanting, be absent, be missing.

dēsuper, *adv.*, from above.

dētineō, tinuī, tentum (2), keep back, detain.

deus, ī, *m.*, *pl.* dei *or* di, god (*sometimes used for* goddess, *as in verse* 632 *of* Venus).

dēvolvō, volvī, volūtum (3), roll down.

dexter, tra, trum, *adj.*, on the right side; dextra, ae, *f.*, right hand.

dīcō, dīxī, dictum (3), say, tell, speak.

dictum, ī, *n.*, word.

dies, ēī, *c.* (in *sing.*), *m.* (in *plur.*) day.

diffugio, ere, fūgī (3), flee in different directions.

dīgero, gessī, gestum (3), arrange, interpret.

dīgnus, a, um, *adj.*, suitable, becoming, worthy, *gov. abl.*

dīgredior, ī, gressus, go away, depart.

dīlēctus, a, um, *adj.*, beloved, dear.

dīripiō, ere, ripuī, reptum, plunder, spoil.

dīrus, a, um, *adj.*, fearful, terrible, dire.

discēdō, cessī, cessum (3), go away, depart.

discō, didicī (*no sup.*) (3), learn.

discors, dis, *adj.*, disagreeing, different.

disiciō, ere, iēcī, iectum, dash to pieces, destroy.

diū, *adv.*, for a long time.

dīva, ae, *f.*, goddess.

dīvellō, vellī *and* vulsī, vulsum (3), tear asunder.

dīversum, ī, *n.*, a different route.

dīversus, a, um, *adj.*, various, of different kinds.

dīves, itis, *adj.*, rich, abounding in.

dīvidō, vīsī, vīsum (3), make a breach through, break through, divide.

dīvīnus, a, um, *adj.*, divine, heavenly.

dīvus, ī, *m.*, a deity (*gen. plur.* dīvūm).

dō, dedī, datum, *inf.* dare (1), give, bestow.

dolor, ōris, *m.*, grief, sorrow.

Dolopes, um, *m.*, a people of Thessaly.

dolus, ī, *m.*, craft, deceit, fraud.

dominor, ātus sum (1), bear rule, be master.

domō, uī, itum (1), tame, subdue.

domus, ūs, *f.*, house, dwelling, home, family.

dōnec, *adv.*, until.

dōnum, ī, *n.*, gift.

Dōricus, a, um, *adj.*, Doric, Grecian.

dracō, ōnis, *m.*, serpent.

dubius, a, um, *adj.*, doubtful, uncertain.

dūcō, dūxī, ductum (3), lead, conduct, prolong (of life).

ductor, ōris, *m.*, leader.

dūdum, *adv.*, lately.

dulcis, e, *adj.*, sweet, pleasant.

dum, *conj.*, until.

duo, ae, o, *num. adj. plur.*, two.

dūrus, a, um, hard.

dux, ucis, *m.*, leader, general.

Dymās, antis, *m.*, father of Hecuba.

E

ecce, *demonstrative adv.*, lo, behold.

edāx, ācis, *adj.*, devouring, consuming.

ēdisserō, uī, ertum (3), speak, relate at length, unfold.

ēdūcō, ūxī, uctum (3), lead out, raise up, erect.

efferō, extulī, ēlātum, *inf.* efferre, bear, carry *or* bring out.

effigiēs, ēī, *f.*, image, statue.

effor, effātus sum (1), speak out, utter.

effugiō, ere, fūgī (3), flee, flee out, escape.

effugium, iī, *n.*, escape.

effulgeō, fulsī (*no sup.*) (2), flash, gleam forth.

effundō, fūdī, fūsum (3), pour forth.

egeō, uī (*no sup.*) (2), need, be in want of (*with abl.*).

ego, meī, *plur.* nōs, *pers. pron.*, I.

ēgredior, i, gressus (3), go out *or* forth.

ei, *interj.*, woe, alas (*with dative*).

ēlābor, ēlāpsus (3), glide out, escape.

ēmicō, uī, ātum (1), move quickly, spring forth.

ēmoveō, mōvī, mōtum (2), move out, remove.

enim, *conj.*, for, indeed.

ēnsis, is, *m.*, sword.

eō, īvī *or* iī, itum, go (*inf.* īre, *pres. part.* iēns, euntis).

Eōus, a, um, *adj.*, of the morning, Eastern.

Epēos, ī, *m.*, the contriver of the wooden horse.

Ēpytus, ī; *m.*, a brave Trojan.

equidem, *adv.*, indeed, truly.

equus, ī, *m.*, horse.

ergō, *adv.*, therefore.

ēripiō, ere, uī, eptum, snatch away.

errō, āvī, ātum (1), wander, stray.

error, ōris, *m.*, wandering, mistake, fraud.

ērubēsco, rubuī (*no sup.*) (3), become red, feel ashamed, respect.

ēruō, uī, utum (3), overthrow, subvert.

Erīnys, yos, *f.*, one of the Furies.

et, *conj.*, and (et ... et, both ... and).

etiam, *conj.*, also, moreover.

etsī, *conj.*, even if, although.

Eurus, ī, *m.*, south-east wind.

Eurypylus, ī, *m.*, a Greek sent by the besiegers of Troy to consult the oracle of Apollo.

ēvādō, āsī, āsum (3), go out, escape.

ēveniō, vēnī, ventum (4), come out, come to pass, happen.

ēvertō, tī, sum (3), turn out, overthrow, ruin.

ēvincō, ēvīcī, ēvictum (3), conquer, vanquish utterly.

ex, *or* ē, *prep.* +*abl.*, out of, from; ex quo, since (648).

exārdēscō, ārsī, ārsum (3), burn, blaze, *or* burst forth.

excēdō, cessī, cessum (3), go forth, quit ; *with abl.* depart from.

excidium, iī, *n.*, destruction, overthrow.

excidō, cidī (*no sup.*) (3), fall out, *or* from, escape.

excīdō, cīdī, cīsum (3), cut off, hew down, destroy.

excitō, āvī, ātum (1), rouse, excite.

exclāmō, āvī, ātum (1), call, cry out, exclaim.

excutiō, ere, cussī, cussum, shake out, rouse, wake up.

exeō, īvī *or* iī, itum, *inf.* īre, go out *or* forth.

exercitus, ûs, *m.,* body of troops, army.

exhālō, āvī, ātum (1), breathe out.

exigō, ēgī, āctum (3), drive out.

exitiālis, e, *adj.,* destructive, fatal.

exitium, iī, *n.,* destruction.

exitus, ûs, *m.,* departure ; *hence* death.

exoptātus, a, um, much desired, longed for.

exorior, ortus (3 *and* 4), rise, spring forth.

expediō, īvī *or* **iī, ītum** (4), extricate, get clear.

expendō, endī, ēnsum (3), weigh out, pay, expiate.

experior, pertus sum (4), try, put to the test.

expleō, ēvī, ētum (2), fill up, satiate.

explicō, uī, ātum *or* **itum,** unfold, explain.

exprōmō, psī, ptum (3), bring out, utter.

exsanguis, e, *adj.,* bloodless, pale.

exscindō, scidī, scissum (3), cut out, destroy, raze to the ground.

exsilium, iī, *n.,* banishment, exile.

exspectō, āvī, ātum (1), look out for, wait for, expect.

exstinguō, stīnxī, stīnctum (3), extinguish, put an end to, kill.

exsultō, āvī, ātum (1), leap up, exult, rejoice exceedingly.

exsuperō, āvī, ātum (1), mount high, tower above.

extemplō, *adv.,* forthwith, at once.

extrā, *prep.* +*acc.,* out, outside of.

extrēmus, a, um, *adj. superl.,* latest, last, extreme.

exuō, uī, ūtum (3), strip off, liberate, free.

exuviae, ārum, *f. plur.,* things stripped off, spoils ; *of snakes* the slough *or* old skin.

F

fabricātor, tōris, *m.,* constructor, builder.

fabricō, āvī, ātum (1), construct, build.

faciēs, ēī, *f.,* form, appearance, figure, face.

facilis, e, *adj.,* easy, light.

faciō, ere, fēcī, factum, do, make.

factum, ī, *n.,* deed, act.

fallō, fefellī, falsum (3), deceive, escape notice of.

falsus, a, um, *adj.,* false, pretended.

fāma, ae, *f.,* fame, report.

famulus, ī, *m.,* servant, attendant.

fās, *n. indecl.,* divine law ; *hence* a lawful, fit, right thing.

fastīgium, iī, projecting point, pinnacle, battlement.

fātālis, e, *adj.,* ordained by fate.

fateor, fassus (2), acknowledge, confess.

fātum, ī, *n.,* destiny, fate.

faux, cis, *f., generally in plur.* **faucēs, ium,** jaws, throat.

fax, facis, *f.,* torch.

fēmineus, a, um, *adj.,* belonging to a woman, female.

fenestra, ae, *f.,* window, breach (*in a wall*).

feriō (*no perf. or sup.*) (4), strike.
ferō, tulī, lātum (*inf.* ferre), *v. irreg.*, bear, carry.
ferrum, ī, *n.*, iron, sword, weapon.
ferus, a, um, *adj.*, cruel, fierce ; *as noun* wild animal (*used of the wooden horse*).
fessus, a, um, wearied, tired out.
festīnō, āvī, ātum (1), hasten.
festus, a, um, *adj.*, festal.
fētus, a, um, pregnant, filled with.
fīdēns, confident, l. 61.
fidēs, eī, *f.*, faith, truth, plighted word.
fīdō, fīsus sum, (3), trust, *gov. dat.*
fīdūcia, ae, *f.*, confidence, trust.
fīdus, a, um, *adj.*, trustworthy, sure, safe.
fīgō, xī, xum (3), fix, fasten, imprint (kisses).
fingō, finxī, fictum (3), form, make. fictus, false, l. 107.
fīnis, is, *f.*, end, termination.
fīō, fierī, factus sum, used as *pass.* of facio, become.
fīrmō, āvī, ātum (1), make strong, confirm, ratify.
fīrmus, a, um, *adj.*, strong, firm.
flāgitō, āvī, ātum (1), demand.
flagrō, āvī, ātum (1), blaze, burn.
flamma, ae, *f.*, flame.
flectō, flexī, flexum (3), bend, influence.
fleō, flēvī, flētum (2), weep.
flētus, ūs, *m.*, weeping, tears.
fluctus, ūs, *m.*, wave.
flūmen, inis, *n.*, river, stream.
fluō. flūxī (3), flow, decline.
foedō, āvī, ātum (1), defile, pollute.

fōns, fontis, *m.*, spring, fountain.
fōr, fātus, *inf.* fārī (1), speak, say.
foris, is, *f.*, door.
formīdō, inis, *f.*, fear, dread.
fors, fortis (only in *nom.* and *abl.*), chance (forte *used adverbially*, by chance) ; l. 139, fors, maybe.
forsitan, *adv.*, perhaps.
fortis, e, *adj.*, brave, bold.
fortūna, ae, *f.*, fortune (*personified*, the goddess Fortune).
frāctus, a, um, *adj.* (*from* frango), broken, weakened.
fragor, ōris, *m.*, crashing, din.
fremitus, ūs, *m.*, a roaring, a roar.
fretum, ī, *n.*, strait.
frīgidus, a, um, *adj.*, cold, chill.
frōns, frondis, *f.*, leaf.
frūstrā, *adv.*, in vain, to no purpose.
frūx, frūgis (*generally in plur.*), *f.*, fruits of the earth.
fuga, ae, *f.*, flight.
fugiō, ere, fūgī, flee ; flee from, escape.
fulgeō, sī (*no sup.*) (2), glitter, shine.
fulmen, inis, *n.*, lightning-flash, thunderbolt.
fulvus, a, um, *adj.*, reddish-yellow, tawny.
fūmō, āvī, ātum (1), smoke, reek.
fūmus, ī, *m.*, smoke.
fundāmentum, ī, *n.*, foundation.
fundō, fūdī, fūsum (3), pour out, rout, put to flight ; *in pass.*, scatter (of persons).

fundus, ĭ, *m.*, bottom.

fūnis, is, *m.*, rope.

fūnus, eris, *n.*, death.

furiō, āvī, ātum (1), enrage, madden.

furō, uī (*no sup.*) (3), rage, rave.

furor, ōris, *m.*, rage, fury, madness.

fūrtim, *adv.*, stealthily, furtively.

futūrus, a, um, *fut. part.* of sum.

G

galea, ae, *f.*, helmet.

gaudeō, gavīsus (2), rejoice.

gaza, ae, *f.*, treasure, riches, wealth.

gelidus, a, um, *adj.*, cold.

geminus, a, um, *adj.*, twin-born, twin.

gemitus, ūs, *m.*, groan.

gener, ĭ, *m.*, son-in-law.

genitor, ōris, *m.*, father.

genetrīx, trīcis, *f.*, mother.

gēns, tis, *f.*, nation, family.

genus, eris, *n.*, race, descent, kind, sort.

gerō, gessī, gestum (3), bear, carry, perform.

glomerō, āvī, ātum (1), assemble, mass together.

gloria, ae, *f.*, glory, renown.

gnātus, -ĭ, *m.*, son.

gradus, ūs, *m.*, step.

Graecī, ōrum, *m.*, Greeks.

Graiī, ōrum, *m.*, Greeks.

Graius, a, um, *adj.*, Grecian.

grāmen, inis, *n.*, grass.

grātēs (generally only in *nom.* and *acc. plur.*), *f.*, thanks.

grātus, a, um, *adj.*, pleasing, delightful.

gravis, e, *adj.*, heavy; heavy with age, feeble.

graviter, *adv.*, heavily.

gravō, āvī, ātum (1), load, weigh down, oppress.

gressus, ūs, *m.*, step.

gurges, itis, *m.*, whirlpool, eddying stream.

H

habeō, uī, itum (2), have, hold, regard.

haereō, haesī, haesum (2), cling to, adhere; remain fixed, l. 654.

hasta, ae, *f.*, spear.

haud, *adv.*, not, not at all.

hauriō, sī, stum (4), draw; *hence*, swallow; devour, l. 600.

hebetō, āvī, ātum (1), make blunt; *hence, of the eyesight*, render dull.

Hector, oris, *m.*, eldest son of Priam and Hecuba. He slew Patroclus the friend of Achilles, and was himself killed by Achilles, who fastened his dead body to a war-chariot and dragged it thrice round the walls of Troy.

Hecuba, ae, *f.*, wife of Priam, and daughter of Dymas.

Hesperius, a, um, Western.

heu, *interj.*, alas.

hīc, haec, hoc, *dem. pron.*, this; hoc, this thing, *plur.* haec, these things.

hīc, *adv.*, here.

hiems, emis, *f.*, winter, storm, tempest.

hinc, *adv.*, hence, from this cause, henceforth.

hodiē, *adv.*, to-day.

homŏ, inis, *c.,* a person; in *plur.* men.

horrendus, a, um, *adj.,* horrible, dreadful.

horreŏ, uĭ (*no sup.*) (2), shudder.

horrēscŏ, horruĭ (*no sup.*) (3), begin to shudder.

horror, ŏris, *m.,* a shuddering with fright, dread.

hortor, ātus sum (1), encourage, exhort.

hostia, ae, *f.,* victim.

hostis, is, *c.,* enemy, foe; stranger, guest.

hūc, *adv.,* hither, here.

humus, ĭ, *f.,* the ground (humĭ, *locative case,* on the ground).

Hypanis, is, *m.,* a Trojan.

I

iaceŏ, uĭ (2), lie down (*especially in death*).

iactŏ, āvĭ, ātum (1) (*frequentative* of iaciŏ) keep throwing, utter (*words*), turn over (*in the mind*).

iactūra, ae, *f.,* hurt, damage, loss.

iaculor, ātus sum (1), hurl, cast (*a javelin*).

iam, *adv.,* now, already, presently (1. 600).

iamdūdum, *adv.,* but lately, forthwith.

iamprĭdem, *adv.,* long since.

iānua, ae, *f.,* door (*of a house*), entrance.

ibi, *adv.,* there.

ictus, ūs, *m.,* stroke, blow.

Ĭda, ae, *f.,* mountain near Troy (celebrated as the spot where Paris adjudged the prize of beauty to Venus).

ignārus, a, um, *adj.* unknowing, ignorant of.

ignis, is, *m.,* fire.

ignōtus, a, um, *adj.,* not known.

Ĭliacus, a, um, *adj.,* Trojan.

Ĭlias, dis, *f.,* a Trojan woman.

ĭlicet, *adv.,* forthwith.

Ĭlium, iĭ, *n.,* another name for Troy.

ille, illa, illud, *dem. pro.,* that.

illĭc, there.

imāgŏ, inis, *f.,* form, appearance, phantom.

imbellis, e, *adj.,* unwarlike, unfit for war.

immānis, e, *adj.,* vast, huge.

immemor, oris, *adj.,* unmindful, regardless.

immēnsus, a, um, *adj.,* huge, immense.

immisceŏ, miscuĭ, mĭxtum (2), mix in, mingle among.

immittŏ, mīsĭ, missum (3), send in; *in pass.* rush, charge.

impello, pulĭ, pulsum (3), drive, urge, incite.

imperium, iĭ, *n.,* dominion, command.

impetus, ūs, *m.,* attack, onset, violence.

impius, a, um, *adj.,* unholy, impious.

impleŏ, ēvĭ, ētum (2), fill up.

implicŏ, uĭ (3), clasp, embrace.

impōnŏ, posuĭ, positum (3), put upon, assign to.

improbus, a, um, *adj.,* wicked, cruel, unjust.

imprōvidus, a, um, *adj.,* unforeseeing, unprepared.

imprōvīsus, a, um, *adj.,* unforeseen.

īmus, a, um, *adj.* (*superl.* of īnferus) lowest ; īmum, i, *n.*, bottom.

in, *prep. with abl.*, in ; *with acc.*, into, against.

incendium, iī, *n.*, conflagration, fire.

incendō, endī, ēnsum (3), set on fire, burn ; fire (*of love*).

inceptum, ī, *n.*, beginning, design, purpose.

incertus, a, um, *adj.*, uncertain, doubtful, ill-aimed.

incidō, cidī (3), fall upon.

incipio, ere, cēpī, ceptum (3), to begin.

inclēmentia, ae, *f.*, mercilessness, cruelty.

inclūdō, ūsī, ūsum (3), shut in, enclose.

inclutus, a, um, *adj.*, famous, renowned.

incolumis, e, *adj.*, safe.

incomitātus, a, um, *adj.*, unaccompanied.

incumbō, cubuī, cubitum (3), lie upon, lean over (*dat.*).

incurrō, currī, or cucurrī, cursum (3), run against, fall in with.

incūsō, āvī, ātum (1), accuse.

inde, *aav.*, after this.

indicium, iī, *n.*, accusation, charge.

indīgnor, ātus sum (1), to be indignant at.

indīgnus, a, um, *adj.*, unworthy (with *abl.*).

indomitus, a, um, *adj.*, unsubdued.

indulgeō, ulsī, ultum (2), indulge in (*dat.*).

induō, uī, ūtum (3), put on, clothe.

inēluctābilis, ē, *adj.*, inevitable.

inermis, e, *adj.*, unarmed.

iners, tis, *adj.*, sluggish, motionless.

īnfandus, a, um, *adj.*, unspeakable, abominable.

īnfēlīx, īcis, *adj.*, unhappy, luckless.

īnfēnsus, a, um, *adj.*, hostile.

īnfestus, a, um, *adj.*, hostile, threatening.

īnfula, ae, *f.*, fillet, band.

ingeminō, āvī, ātum (1), redouble, repeat.

ingēns, entis, *adj.*, huge, mighty.

ingrātus, a, um, *adj.*, unpleasant, unwelcome.

ingruō, uī (3), rush towards, rush against.

iniciō, ere, iēcī, iectum (3), throw in, against, *with pers. pron. as object*, rush into.

inimīcus, a, um, *adj.*, unfriendly, hostile.

inīquus, a, um, *adj.*, unfavourable, adverse.

inlābor, lāpsus (3), glide into.

inlūdō, sī, sum (3), mock (*dat.*).

innoxius, a, um, *adj.*, harmless.

innūptus, a, um, *adj.*, unmarried.

inquam, *v. defect.*, say (3*rd pers.* inquit).

inritus, a, um, *adj.*, vain, ineffectual.

inruō, ruī (3), rush upon, rush into.

īnsānia, ae, *f.*, madness, folly.

īnsānus, a, um, *adj.*, mad, desperate.

īnscius, a, um, *adj.*, ignorant of.

īnsequor, secūtus (3), follow, pursue.

īnsertō (1), *frequentative* of īnserō, insert.

īnsideō, sēdī, sessum (2), seat oneself upon.

īnsidiae, ārum, *f. plur.*, ambush; stratagem, treachery.

īnsīgne, is, *n.*, distinctive mark, ornament.

īnsinuō, āvī, ātum (1), penetrate.

īnsonō, uī, itum (1), resound.

īnsōns, tis, *adj.*, innocent.

īnspiciō, ere, spēxī, spectum (3), look into, examine.

īnstār, *n. indecl.*, a likeness of, as large as (with *gen.*).

īnstaurō, āvī, ātum (1), repair, restore.

īnsternō, strāvī, strātum (3), spread over, cover.

īnstō, stitī, statum (1), press on, hurry forward.

īnstruō, ūxī, ūctum (3), draw up (*troops or ships*).

īnsula, ae, *f.*, island.

īnsultō, āvī, ātum (1), leap upon, exult.

īnsuper, *adv.*, over and above, moreover.

integer, gra, grum, *adj.*, untouched, sound, fresh.

intemerātus, a, um, *adj.*, undefiled.

intendō, endī, ēnsum or entum (3), stretch upon.

intentus, a, um, *adj.*, stretched out, eager, intent.

inter, *prep.* with *acc.*, between, among.

interclūdō, sī, sum (3), hinder, prevent.

intereā, *adv.*, meanwhile.

interior, ius, *adj.*, inner.

intexō, texuī, textum (3), interweave.

intonō, uī (1), thunder.

intorqueō, torsī, tortum (2), hurl against (*dat.*).

intrā, *prep.* with *acc.* within.

intus, *adv.*, within.

inultus, a, um, *adj.*, unavenged.

inūtilis, e, *adj.*, useless.

invādō, vāsī, vāsum (3), attack, fall upon.

inveniō, vēnī, ventum (4), find.

inventor, ōris, *m.*, deviser.

invidia, ae, *f.*, envy.

invīsus, a, um, *adj.*, hateful.

invītus, a, um, *adj.*, unwilling.

involvō, volvī, volūtum (3), enshroud.

Īphitus, ī, *n.*, a Trojan, comrade of Aeneas.

ipse, ipsa, ipsum, *dem. pron.*, self.

īra, ae, *f.*, anger, wrath.

iste, ista, istud, *dem. pron.*, that (of yours).

ita, *adv.*, in this fashion, thus.

iter, itineris, *n.*, journey, road, way.

iterum, *adv.*, again, a second time.

Ithacus, a, um, *adj.*, belonging to Ithaca, an island in the Ionian Sea; once the Kingdom of Ulysses.

iuba, ae, *f.*, mane, crest (*of a dragon, helmet, etc.*).

iubeō, iussī, iussum (2), order, command.

iugum, ī, n., yoke, mountain, ridge, peak.

Iūlus, ī, m., see Ascanius.

iūnctūra, ae, f., joint.

iungō, iūnxī, iūnctum (3), join, unite.

Iūnō, ōnis, f., wife of Jupiter, daughter of Saturn.

Iūpiter, Iovis, m., Jupiter, Jove (king of the gods, son of Saturn).

iūs, iūris, n., right, justice; in plur. laws.

iussum, ī, n., order, command.

iussū, at the command of, with gen.

iūstus, a, um, adj., just.

iuvenīlis, e, adj., youthful, of one's youth.

iūvenis, is, adj., young, youthful; as a noun, young person.

iuventa, ae, f., youth (the state of).

iuventus, ūtis, f., youth; collectively, the young men.

iūvō, iūvī, iūtum (1), please, delight.

iuxtā, adv., close to, hard by.

L

lābēs, is, f., blot, taint.

labō, āvī, ātum (1), totter.

labor, ōris, m., labour, toil, trouble, distress.

lābor, lāpsus (3), glide, slip, fall.

Lacaena, ae, adj., Spartan (as noun, a Spartan woman).

lacrima, ae, f., tear.

lacrimō, āvī, ātum (1), shed tears.

lacus, ūs, m., lake, pool.

laedō, laesī, laesum (3), hurt, injure.

laetus, a, um, adj., joyful, prosperous, luxuriant (of crops).

laevum, adv., on the left hand.

laevus, a, um, adj., left, on the left side; laeva, left hand, l. 552.

lambō, ? (no sup.) (3), lick.

lāmentābīlis, e, adj., deplorable, pitiable.

Lāocoōn, ontis, m., priest of Apollo, who with his two sons was devoured by the serpents of Pallas.

lāpsō, āvī, ātum (1) (frequentative from lābor), slip, stumble.

lāpsus, ūs, m., gliding.

largus, a, um, adj., plentiful.

Lārissaeus, a, um, adj., of Larissa, a town of ancient Thessaly, on the river Peneus.

lassus, a, um, adj., wearied, tired.

lātē, adv., far and wide.

latebra, ae, f., lurking-place.

lateō, uī (no sup.) (2), lie hid.

lātus, a, um, adj., wide, broad.

laudō, āvī, ātum (1), praise.

laurus, ī and ūs, f., laurel-tree.

laus, laudis, f., commendation, praise.

laxō, āvī, ātum (1), loosen, release.

legō, lēgī, lēctum (3), gather, collect, traverse (the sea).

lēnis, e, adj., smooth, calm, gentle.

leō, ōnis, m., lion.

lētum, ĭ, *n.*, death.

levis, e, *adj.*, light, swift.

levō, āvī, ātum (1), make light, remove, relieve.

lex, lēgis, *f.*, law.

lignum, ĭ, *n.*, wood, firewood.

ligō, āvī, ātum (1), surround, bind.

līmen, inis, *n.*, threshold, door.

līmes, itis, *m.*, track, path.

līmōsus, a, um, *adj.*, muddy.

lĭngua, ae, *f.*, tongue.

ᴵnquō, līquī (*no sup.*) (3), to leave.

litō, āvī, ātum (1), to obtain favourable omeᴜ..

lītus, oris, *n.*, sea-shore, beach.

loco, āvī, ātum, to place.

locus, ĭ, *m.*, a place, position; (*plur.* locī and loca).

longaevus, a, um, *adj.*, aged.

longē, *adv.*, afar off.

longus, a, um, *adj.*, long.

loquor, locūtus (3), to speak.

lōrum, ĭ, *n.*, thong, rein.

lūbricus, a, um, *adj.*, slippery, smooth.

Lūcifer, erī, *m.*, morning-star.

lūctus, ūs, *m.*, wailing, grief, lament.

lūmen, inis, *n.*, light, life, eye.

lūna, ae, *f.*, moon.

lupus, ĭ, *m.*, wolf.

lūstrō, āvī, ātum (1), purify, survey, examine, observe, traverse.

lūx, lūcis, *f.*, light, brightness.

Lȳdius, a, um, *adj.*, belonging to Lydia (a country of Asia Minor, from which the Etrurians were said to have come).

M

Machāon, onis, *m.*, son of Aesculapius, a Greek warrior and surgeon.

māchina, ae, *f.*, a machine (*of any kind*), contrivance.

macto, āvī, ātum (1), slay, sacrifice.

maestus, a, um, *adj.*, sad.

magis, *adv.*, more; magis atque magis, more and more.

māgnus, a, um, *adj.*, large, great.

māior, us, *adj.*, comparative of māgnus.

male, *adv.*, badly; male amīcus, unfriendly; male fīdus, untrustworthy.

malus, a, um, *adj.*, bad, unfortunate, hurtful (*as noun*, malum, ĭ, *n.*, misfortune).

maneō, mānsī, mānsum (2); remain, continue; wait for, abide.

manica, ae, *f.*, handcuff.

manifestus, a, um, *adj.*, evident.

manus, ūs, *f.*, hand; band.

Mārs, Mārtis, *m.*, god of war; war.

māter, tris, *f.*, mother.

māximus, a, um, *adj. superl.* of māgnus, great.

mēcum (for cum me), with me.

medius, a, um, *adj.*, middle.

melior, us, *adj.* (*comp.* of bonus), better.

meminī, remember (*inf.* meminisse; *imperative* mementō).

memorābilis, e, *adj.*, memorable.

memorō, āvī, ātum (1), relate.

mendāx, ācis, *adj.*, untruthful, lying.

mēne, mē, *pers. pron.* with *interrogative particle* ne.

Menelāus, ī, *m.*, son of Atreus (brother of Agamemnon, husband of Helen).

mēns, mentis, *f.*, the mind.

mēnsa, ae, *f.*, table.

mentior, mentītus (4), declare falsely, lie.

mercor, ātus sum (1), to traffic, buy.

mereō, uī, itum (2), deserve.

mereor, meritus sum (2), deserve.

metus, ūs, *m.*, fear.

meus, a, um, *poss. pron.*, mine.

micō, uī (*no sup.*) (1), gleam, shine.

mīles, itis, *m.*, soldier.

mīlle, *num. adj. indecl.*, thousand (*as noun in plur.* mīlia, *gen.* mīlium, *n.*).

Minerva, ae, *f.*, Minerva, goddess of wisdom.

minister, trī, *m.*, servant, attendant, abettor.

minor, ātus sum (1), threaten.

mīrābilis, e, *adj.*, wonderful.

mīror, ātus sum (1), admire, wonder at.

misceō, miscuī, mixtum (2), mix, disturb, confuse, stir up.

miser, a, um, *adj.*, sad, wretched.

miserābilis, e, *adj.*, pitiable, wretched.

misereor, eritus sum (2), pity (*with gen.*).

miserēscō (*no perf. or sup.*) (3), pity.

miserrimus, a, um, *adj. superl. of* miser.

mittō, mīsī, missum (3), send.

modo, *adv.*, only.

moenia, ium, *n. plur.*, walls, fortifications.

mōlēs, is, *f.*, a huge mass, a great structure.

mōlior, ītus sum (4), undertake.

mollis, e, *adj.*, soft.

moneō, uī, itum (2), advise, warn.

mōns, tis, *m.*, mountain.

mōnstrō, āvī, ātum (1), show, point out.

mōnstrum, ī, *n.*, omen, monster.

montānus, a, um, of the mountain ; mountain *as adj.*

mora, ae, *f.*, delay.

morior, morī, mortuus (3), die.

moritūrus, a, um, *fut. part.* of morior.

moror, ātus sum (1), delay.

mors, tis, *f.*, death.

morsus, ūs, *m.*, bite.

mortālis, e, *adj.*, mortal (as *subs.* mortālis, is, *m.*, a human being).

moveō, mōvī, mōtum (2), move, excite.

mūcrō, ōnis, *m.*, point, sword.

mūgītus, ūs, *m.*, bellowing.

multō, *adv.*, by much.

multus, a, um, *adj.*, much.

mūrus, ī, *m.*, wall.

mūtō, āvī, ātum (1), change, alter.

Mycēnae, ārum, *f.*, Mycenae, a city of Argolis, of which Agamemnon was king.

Mygdonidēs, ae, *m.*, Coroebus, ~~son~~ of Mygdon, Trojan

l

N

nam, *conj.*, for.

namque, *conj.*, for.

narrō, narrāvī, narrātum (1), tell, relate.

nāscor, nātus sum (3), to be born.

nāta, ae, *f.*, daughter.

nātus, ī, *m.*, son (*in plur.* nātī, children, of either sex).

nāvis, is, *f.*, ship.

nē, *conj.*, that not, lest.

ne, *enclitic* and *interrogative particle*.

nebula, ae, *f.*, mist, vapour.

nec *or* neque, *conj.*, and not (neque ... neque, neither ... nor).

nefas, *n. indecl.*, impiety, impious.

Neoptolemus, ī, *m.*, Neoptolemus, son of Achilles.

nepos, -ōtis, *m.*, descendant.

Neptūnius, a, um, *adj.*, of Neptune, Neptunian.

Neptūnus, ī, *m.*, Neptune.

nēquīquam, *adv.*, in vain, to no purpose.

Nēreūs, eī *or* eos, Nereus, a sea-deity.

nesciō, scīvī *or* sciī, scītum (4), not know; nesciō quod, I know not what; nesciō quis, some one *or* other.

neu (contracted form of neve), *conj.* not, nor.

nex, necis, *f.*, death, murder.

nī, *conj.* if not, unless.

nihil, *indecl. n.*, nothing; *used adverbially*, in no respect.

nimbus, ī, *m.*, rain-storm, thunder-cloud.

nitidus, **a, um,** *adj.*, shining, bright.

nītor, nīsus or nīxus sum (3), lean, climb, exert oneself, endeavour.

nōdus, ī, *m.*, knot.

nōmen, inis, *n.*, name, reputation.

nōn, *adv.*, not.

noster, tra, trum, *poss. pron.* our.

Notus, ī, *m.*, south wind.

nōtus, a, um, *adj.*, well-known.

novus, a, um, new, fresh.

nox, noctis, *f.*, night.

nūbēs, is, *f.*, cloud.

nūdus, a, um, *adj.*, bare, uncovered.

nūllus, a, um, *adj.*, no, not any (*gen.* nūllīus; *dat.* nūllī).

nūmen, inis, *n.*, *literally*, nodding (in reference to the oracular responses); *hence*, divine will *or* power, deity.

numerus, ī, *m.*, number.

numquam, *adv.*, never.

nunc, *adv.*, now.

nūntius, iī, *m.*, messenger.

nurus, ūs, *f.*, daughter-in-law.

nusquam, *adv.*, nowhere.

nūtō, āvī, ātum (1), nod, sway to and fro, totter to its fall (*of a tree*).

O

ō, *interj.*, O, oh.

ob, *prep.* + *acc.*, on account of.

obdūcō, dūxī, ductum (3), spread over, cover.

obiectō, āvī, ātum (1), expose.

ōbiciō, ere, iēcī, iectum, expose (to the enemy); thrust upon (l. 200) oblīvīscor, oblītus sum (3), forget (*with genitive*).

obruō, ruī, rutum (3), overthrow, overwhelm.

obscūrus, a, um, *adj.*, dark, gloomy.

observō, āvī, ātum (1), watch, observe, guard.

obsideō, ēdī, essum (2), besiege, invest, blockade.

obstupēscō, stupuī (3), become amazed.

obtegō, tēxī, tēctum (3), cover over, conceal.

obtruncō, āvī, ātum (1), slaughter, slay.

occāsus, ūs, *m.*, fall, ruin, destruction.

occidō, cidī, cāsum, fall, perish.

occultō, āvī, ātum (1), hide, conceal.

occumbō, cubuī, cubitum (3), lie down, yield (*with dat.*); fall victim.

Ōceanus, ī, *m.*, Ocean.

oculus, ī, *m.*, eye.

ōdī, *inf.* ōdisse, hate.

odium, iī, *n.*, hatred, ill-will.

offerō, obtulī, oblātum, *inf.* offerre, bring towards (*with reflexive pron.*), to present oneself.

Olympus, ī, *m.*, Olympus, mountain on the borders of Macedonia and Thessaly, fabled abode of the gods.

ōmen, inis, *n.*, augury, omen.

omnipotēns, entis, *adj.*, all-powerful, omnipotent.

omnis, e, *adj.*, all (omnēs, all persons; omnia, all things).

onus, eris, *n.*, burden, load.

opācus, a, um, *adj.*, shady.

opīmus, a, um, *adj.*, rich, fertile.

oppōnō, posuī, positum (3), place against, lay open to.

ops, opis, *f.* (*nom. sing.* does not occur), power, strength; *plur.* opēs, *gen.* opum, wealth, resources, means, help.

optō, āvī, ātum (1), wish, desire.

opus, eris, *n.*, work, employment.

ōra, ae, *f.*, coast, country.

ōrāculum, ī, *n.*, oracle.

orbis, is, *m.*, circle (*of a shield*), coil (*of a serpent*).

Orcus, ī, *m.*, the lower world.

ordior, ōrsus sum (4), begin.

ordō, inis, *m.*, row, line, class, rank.

orior, ortus sum (4), rise, arise.

ōrnus, ī, *f.*, mountain-ash.

ōrō, āvī, ātum (1), implore, entreat, pray.

ōs, ōris, *n.*, mouth, face; in *plur.* speech.

ōs, ossis, *n.*, bone.

ōsculum, ī, *n.*, kiss.

ostendō, endī, ēnsum (3), to show.

Othryadēs, ae, *m.*, son of Othrys, i.e. Panthus, Trojan priest of Apollo.

P

Palamēdēs, is, *m.*, son of Nauplius, King of Euboea.

Palladium, iī, *n.*, image of Pallas Athene, said to have fallen from heaven. The safety of Troy was supposed to depend upon it; it was carried off by Ulysses and Diomede.

Pallas, adis, *f.*, Pallas Athene, Greek goddess identified by the Romans with Minerva.

palma, ae, *f.*, palm (*of the hand*).

palūs, ūdis, *f.*, swamp, marsh.

pandō, pandī, pānsum *and* **passum,** spread out, open ; **crīnibus passīs,** with dishevelled hair.

Panthūs, see **Othryades.**

par, paris, *adj.*, equal to (*with dat.*).

parātus, a, um, *adj.*, ready.

parcō, pepercī, parsum (3), spare, curb (with *dat.*).

parēns, entis, parent.

pāreō, uī, itum (2), obey (*with dat.*).

pariēs, etis, *m.*, wall (of a house).

pariō, ere, peperī, partum, bring forth, obtain.

Paris, idis, *m.*, Paris, son of Priam and Hecuba. He carried off Helen, and so was the cause of the Trojan war.

pariter, *adv.*, equally, together, at the same time.

parma, ae, *f.*, small shield.

parō, āvī, ātum (1), prepare, make ready.

pars, tis, *f.*, part, portion.

parvus, a, um, *adj.*, small, little.

pāscor, pāstus sum (3), feed upon.

passim, *adv.*, all along, in every direction.

passus, a, um, *perf. part. pass.* of **pando** *or* **patior.**

passus, ūs, *m.*, step.

pāstus, a, um, *perf. part.* of **pāscor.**

patefaciō, ere, fēcī, factum, open, explain.

pateō, uī (*no sup.*) (2), lie open.

pater, tris, *m.*, father.

patēscō, patuī (*no sup.*), to become plain.

patior, passus sum (3), suffer, endure.

patria, ae, *f.*, fatherland, native country.

patrius, a, um, *adj.*, belonging to a father, belonging to one's country ; native, ll. 95, 279.

paulātim, *adv.*, little by little, by degrees.

pauper, eris, *adj.*, poor.

pavidus, a, um, *adj.*, fearful, frightened.

pavitō, āvī, ātum (1), tremble with fear.

pavor, ōris, *m.*, fear, dread.

pectus, oris, *n.*, breast, heart ; mind.

pelagus, ī, n., the sea.

Pelasgī, ōrum, *m.*, Pelasgi, the oldest inhabitants of Greece ; the Greeks.

Pelasgus, a, um, *adj.*, Pelasgan, i.e. Greek.

Peliās, ae, *m.*, a Trojan, comrade of Aeneas.

Pēlīdēs, ae, *m.*, son or grandson of Peleus, i.e. Achilles or Neoptolemus.

pellāx, ācis, *adj.*, seductive, deceitful.

pellis, is, *f.*, skin, hide.

pellō, pepulī, pulsum (3), drive away.

Pelopēus, a, um, *adj.*, of Pelops ; Grecian.

Penātēs, ium, *m.*, the Penates, household gods.

pendeō, pependī (*no sup.*) (2), hang from.

Pēneleus, eī, *m.*, Peneleus, leader of the Boeotians in the Trojan war.

penetrāle, is, *n.*, inner part of a building, sanctuary.

penitus, *adv.*, far within, completely.

per, *prep.* +*acc.*, through, by means of.

pereō, īvī *or* iī, itum, perish.

pererrō, āvī, ātum (1), wander over, traverse.

perfundō, fūdī, fūsum (3), wet through.

Pērgama, ōrum, *n.*, the citadel of Troy.

perīclum, ī, *n.*, danger, peril.

Periphās, antis, *m.*, Periphas, companion of Pyrrhus.

peritūrus, a, um, *fut. part.* of pereō.

periūrus, a, um, *adj.*, swearing falsely, perjured.

perrumpō, rūpī, ruptum (3), break through.

persolvō, solvī, solūtum (3), pay in full; persolvere grātēs, to return thanks.

perstō, stitī, stātum (1), continue, persevere.

perveniō, vēnī, ventum (4), reach, arrive at; (*used impersonally in pass.* perventum est, had reached *or* arrived at).

pervius, a, um, *adj.*, passable.

pēs, pedis, *m.*, foot; ferre pedem, to go.

petō, īvī *or* iī, ītum (3), seek, proceed to, desire, strive after.

phalanx, ngis, *f.*, phalanx, host.

Phoebus, ī, *m.*, poetical name for Apollo.

Phoenīx, īcis, *m.*, son of Amyntor and friend of Achilles.

Phryges, um, *m.*, Phrygians, a people of Asia Minor in whose country Troy was.

Phrygius, a, um, *adj.*, Phrygian.

pietās, ātis, *f.*, piety, filial affection.

pīneus, a, um, *adj.*, made of pine *or* fir.

piō, āvī, ātum (1), make atonement for, expiate.

placeō, uī, itum (2), please (*with dat.*).

plācō, āvī, ātum (1), pacify, appease.

plangor, ōris, *m.*, wailing, lamentation.

plūrimus, a, um, *adj.* (*superl. of* multus), very much, very great, very many.

poena, ae, *f.*, satisfaction (*for an offence*) ; dare poenās, to suffer punishment; sūmere poenās, to inflict punishment.

Polītēs, ae, *m.*, Polites, a son of Priam, slain by Pyrrhus in the sight of his parents.

polus, ī, *m.*, the heavens.

pōne, *adv.*, behind.

pōnō, posuī, positum (3), place, put *or* lay down, cast aside.

pontus, ī, *m.*, the sea.

populus, ī, *m.*, people.

porta, ae, *f.*, door, gate.

porticus, ūs, *f.*, porch, colonnade.

portō, āvī, ātum (1), carry.

poscō, poposcī (*no sup.*) (3), demand.

positus, a, um, *see* pōnō.

possum, potuī (*inf.* posse, *pres. part.* potēns), be able.

post, (*adv.*) afterwards ; (*prep.* +*acc.*) after, behind.

postis, is, *m.*, post, doorpost.

postquam, *adv.*, when.

praeceps, cipitis, *adj.*, headlong, rapid.

praeceptum, ī, *n.*, instruction, order, warning (l. 345).

praecipitō, āvī, ātum, rush headlong ; throw headlong.

praecipuē, *adv.*, especially.

praecordia, ōrum, *n. plur.*, breast, heart.

praeda, ae, *f.*, spoil, booty.

praemetuēns, *pres. part.* of praemetuō, dreading.

praemium, iī, *n.*; recompense, reward.

prehendō, endī, ēnsum (3), lay hold of, grasp.

premō, pressī, pressum (3), press.

prēndō, prēndī, prēnsum (3), seize, grasp, lay hold of.

prēnsō, āvī, ātum (1), grasp tightly.

prex, precis, *f.*, prayer (*not found in nom. sing.*).

Priameius, a, um, *adj.*, belonging to Priam, of Priam.

Priamus, ī, *m.*, Priam, King of Troy.

prīmum, *adv.*, firstly, for the first time.

prīmus, a, um, *adj.* first, foremost.

prīncipiō, *adv.*, in the beginning.

prius, *adv.*, sooner ; first, l. 596.

prō, *prep.* +*abl.*, in place of, for.

prōcēdō, cessī, cessum (3), advance.

procul, *adv.*, far off, at a distance.

prōcumbō, cubuī, cubitum (3), fall forwards, fall down.

prōditiō, ōnis, *f.*, betraying, treachery.

prōdō, didī, ditum (3), betray.

prōdūcō, dūxī, ductum (3), prolong.

proelium, iī, *n.*, battle, fight.

prōlābor, lāpsus sum (3), glide forward, tumble ; fall headlong, l. 555

prōmissum, ī, *n.*, promise.

prōmittō, mīsī, missum (3), promise.

prōmō, psī, ptum (3), take forth ; se promere, come forth.

propinquō, āvī, ātum (1), draw near, approach.

propinquus, a, um, *adj.*, near, allied ; propinquī, neighbours.

propius, *adv.*, nearer.

prōsequor, secūtus sum (3), follow on, proceed.

prōspiciō, ere, ēxī, ectum, look forward.

prōtegō, tēxī, tēctum (3), cover, defend, protect.

prōtinus, *adv.*, forthwith, immediately.

prōtrahō, trāxī, tractum (3), drag forth.

prōvehō, vēxī, vectum (3), carry forward ; se provehere, proceed, advance.

proximus, a, um, *adj.*, nearest, next to, *superl.* of prope.

pūbēs, is, *f.*, youth, young folk.

puella, ae, *f.*, girl, maiden.

puer, ĭ, *m.*, boy.

pūgna, ae, *f.*, battle.

pulcher, chra, chrum, *adj.*, beautiful, honourable.

pulvis, eris, *m.*, dust.

puppis, is, *f.*, stern ; ship.

pūrus, a, um, *adj.*, pure, clear, bright.

putō, āvī, ātum (1), think, suppose.

Pyrrhus, *see* Neoptolemus.

Q

quā, *adv.*, where.

quaerō, sīvī, sītum (3), seek, ask.

quālis, e, *adj.* *interrogative*, of what kind ; *relative*, of such a kind as.

quamquam, although.

quandō, *adv.*, when.

quantum, *adv.*, how much.

quantus, a, um, *adj.*, as great as, how great.

quater, *adv.*, four times.

quatiō, ere, quassum, shake.

que, *conj.* (*enclitic*), and ; que ... que, both ... and.

quĭ, quae, quod, *gen.* cuius, *dat.* cui, *rel. pron.*, who, which.

quia, *conj.*, because.

quĭcumque, quaecumque, quodcumque, *relat. pron.*, whosoever.

quid, *adv.*, why.

quidem, *adv.*, indeed.

quiēs, ētis, *f.*, rest, repose.

quĭn etiam, *conj.*, moreover, yea too.

quīnī, ae, a, *distributive adj.*, five apiece.

quīnquāgintā, *num. adj. indecl.*, fifty.

quis, quae, quid, *inter. pron.*, who, what.

quisquam, quicquam *or* quidquam, *indef. pron.*, any one *or* thing.

quisquis, quidquid *or* quicquid, *indef. pron.*, whoever, whatever.

quō, *adv.*, whither.

quod, *conj.*, because, inasmuch as.

quōnam, *adv.*, whither.

quondam, *adv.*, once, formerly, at times.

quoque, *conj.*, also, too.

quot, *num. adj. indecl.*, how many, (as many) as.

R

rabiēs, iem, iē, *f.* (*not found in other cases*), madness, rage, violence.

rapidus, a, um, *adj.*, swift, rushing.

rapio, ere, uĭ, ptum, carry off, plunder.

raptō, āvī, ātum (1), drag violently.

raptor, ōris, *m.*, a ravager, plunderer ; *as adj.*, ravening.

ratiō, ōnis, *f.*, judgment, reason.

raucus, a, um, *adj.*, hoarse, hollow-sounding.

recēdō, cessī, cessum (3), stand back, withdraw.

recēns, entis, *adj.*, fresh, recent.

recipiō, ere, cēpī, ceptum, take back, receive.

recondō, condidī, conditum (3), hide, conceal.

recūsō, āvī, ātum (1), refuse, decline.

recutiō, ere, cussī, cussum, strike back, cause to rebound.

reddō, didī, ditum (3), give back, restore.

redeō, īvī *or* iī, itum, *inf.* redīre, go *or* come back, return.

reditus, ūs, *m.*, return.

redūcō, dūxī, ductum (3), lead back.

referō, rettulī, relātum, *inf.* referre, bring back, relate; se referre, return ; *pass.*, flow back, l. 169.

reflectō, flēxī, flexum (3), bend *or* turn back.

refugiō, ere, fūgī, flee back, recoil.

refulgeō, fulsī (*no sup.*) (2), flash back (the light); shine, l. 590.

rēgīna, ae, *f.*, queen.

regiō, ōnis, *f.*, direction, line, region.

rēgius, a, um, *adj.*, royal.

rēgnātor, ōris, *m.*, ruler.

rēgnum, ī, *n.*, kingdom.

rēligiō, ōnis, *f.*, religion, religious feeling, an object of religious veneration.

rēligiōsus, a, um, holy, sacred.

relinquō, līquī, lictum (3), leave behind, forsake.

relūceō, lūxī (*no sup.*) (2), shine back, flash.

remeō, āvī, ātum (1), go back, return.

remētior, mēnsus sum (4), measure back (*perf. part. with pass. force*, repassed, retraced).

remittō, mīsī, missum (3), send back.

renovō, āvī, ātum (1), renew.

reor, ratus sum (2), suppose, think (*inf.* rērī).

repellō, reppulī, repulsum (3), drive back.

rependō, endī, ēnsum (3), pay back.

repentē, *adv.*, suddenly.

repetō, īvī *or* iī, ītum (3), seek again, fetch back.

repleō, ēvī, ētum (2), fill.

reportō, āvī, ātum (1), carry back, report.

reposcō (*no perf. or sup.*) (3), demand in return, claim.

reprimō, pressī, pressum (3), hold back, restrain.

requiēscō, ēvī, ētum (3), rest.

requīrō, quīsīvī, quīsītum (3), seek again, demand back, inquire.

rēs, reī, *f.*, thing, property.

resideō, sēdī, sessum (2), sit behind, stay behind.

resistō, stitī (*no sup.*) (3), oppose, withstand.

resolvō, solvī, solūtum (3), let loose, disclose, reveal.

rēspiciō, ere, spēxī, spectum, look back, look back for.

respōnsum, ī, *n.*, answer, reply.

rēstinguō, īnxī, īnctum (3), put out, extinguish.

rēstō, stitī (*no sup.*) (1), stand behind, remain.

retrō, *adv.*, back, backwards.

revertor, reversus (3), go back, return.

revinciō, vīnxī, vīnctum (4), bend, back.

revīsō (no *perf.* or *sup.*) (3), visit again.

revolvō, volvī, volūtum (3), roll back, dwell upon.

rēx, rēgis, *m.*, king.

Rlpheus, eI, m., Ripheus, comrade of Aeneas.

rōbur, oris, n., oak-tree, timber; the wooden horse (as being made of oak), strength.

rogo, āvī, ātum (1), ask.

roseus, a, um, adj., rosy.

rota, ae, f., wheel.

ruīna, ae, f., downfall, ruin.

rumpō, rūpī, ruptum (3), break, burst, burst forth (of a storm) ; **rumpere vōcem,** to utter a sound.

ruō, I, itum (3), fall down (in ruins), rush.

rūrsus, adv., back again, a second time.

S

sacer, cra, crum, adj., sacred.

sacerdōs, dōtis, c., priest or priestess.

sacrō, āvī, ātum (1), consecrate.

saepe, adv., often.

saepius, adv. comparative of saepe.

saeviō, iī, ītum (4), to be fierce, rage.

saevus, a, um, adj., fierce, savage, cruel.

salsus, a, um, adj., salted.

saltus, ūs, m., a leap, a spring.

salum, ī, n., the sea.

salūs, ūtis, f., health, safety.

sanctus, a, um, adj., holy, sacred.

sanguineus, a, um, blood-coloured, blood-stained.

sanguis, inis, m., blood, race, stock.

saniēs, ēī, f., gore.

sata, ōrum, n. plur., crops.

satiō, āvī, ātum (1), satisfy.

satis (or sat), adv., sufficiently, enough.

saucius, a, um, adj., wounded.

saxum, ī, n., stone, rock.

Scaeus, a, um, adj., Scaean ; **portae Scaeae,** the western gate of Troy.

scālae, ārum, f. plur., steps, a ladder.

scandō, scandī, scānsum (3), climb, mount.

scelerātus, a, um, adj., accursed, impious.

scelus, eris, n., wicked deed, crime, guilt.

scīlicet, adv., forsooth.

scindō, scidī, scissum (3), di vide, part.

scītātum, supine from scītor.

scītor, ātus sum (1), inquire, consult.

Scȳrius, a, um, adj., belonging to Scyros, an island in the Aegean Sea. Here Achilles retired to avoid going to the war, and was concealed by the King Lycomedes.

se, reflexive pron., 3rd pers., himself, themselves, etc.

seco, cuī, ctum (1), cut.

sēcrētus, a, um, adj., separated, retired, apart.

sēcum, for cum sē, see cum.

secundus, a, um, adj., favourable, fortunate, heartening (l. 617).

secūris, is, f., axe.

secus, adv., otherwise.

sed conj., but.

sedeō, sēdī, sessum (2), sit ; be settled, l. 660.

sēdēs, is, *f.*, seat, dwelling-place, abode, place.

seges, etis, *f.*, corn-field, corn-crop.

sēgnitiēs, ēī, *f.*, slowness, laziness.

semper, *adv.*, always.

senior, ōris, *m.* (*comparative of* senex, *used as a noun*), an old man.

sententia, ae, *f.*, opinion.

sentiō, sēnsī, sēnsum (4), perceive, be aware of.

sentis, is, *m.*, thorn, briar.

sepeliō, sepelīvī *or* iī, sepultum (4), bury.

septem, *num. adj. indecl.*, seven.

sepulcrum, ī, *n.*, tomb, sepulchre.

sequor, secūtus sum (3), follow.

serēnus, a, um, *adj.*, calm.

serō, sēvī, satum (3), sow, beget (satus, *perf. part. pass., with abl.* descended from).

serpēns, tis, *c.*, snake.

serpō, psī, ptum (3), creep.

sērus, a, um, *adj.*, late.

servāns, tis, *pres. part. of* servo, *with gen.* observant of, attentive to.

serviō, īvī *or* iī, ītum (4), be a slave to, serve, *with dat.*

servō, āvī, ātum (1), preserve, protect.

sēsē, reduplicated form of sē, *reflexive pron.*

seu, *conj.*, see sīve.

sī, *conj.*, if.

sībilus, a, um, *adj.*, hissing.

sīc, *adv.*, so, in this way.

siccus, a, um, *adj.*, dry.

sīdus, eris, *n.*, star.

Sīgēus, a, um, belonging to Sigeum, a promontory of Troas, the country around Troy.

sīgno, āvī, ātum (1), mark, point out.

sīgnum, ī, *n.*, sign, token.

silentium, iī, *n.*, silence, stillness.

sileō, uī (*no sup.*) (2), be silent.

silva, ae, *f.*, a wood.

similis, e, *adj.*, like.

simul, *adv.*, at once, at the same time.

simulācrum, ī, *n.*, image, effigy, ghost.

simulō, āvī, ātum (1), to feign, to pretend.

sīn, *conj.*, if on the contrary.

sine, *prep.* +*abl.*, without.

sinistra, ae, *f.*, the left hand.

sinō, sīvī, situm (3), allow, suffer.

Sīnōn, ōnis, *m.*, Sinon, the impostor who induced the Trojans to take the wooden horse into Troy.

sinuō, āvī, ātum (1), bend, curve.

sinus, ūs, *m.*, bay, harbour, gulf.

sī quī, qua, quid, *indef. adj.*, if any.

sī quis, quid, *indef. pron.*, if any one *or* thing.

sistō, stitī, statum (3), set, place.

sīve, *conj.*, or (sīve ... sīve, whether ... or).

socer, erī, *m.*, father-in-law ; *pl.* socerī, parents-in-law.

socius, iī, *m.*, friend, comrade.

socius, a, um, *adj.*, allied.

sōl, sōlis, *m.*, the sun.

soleō, solitus sum (2), be accustomed.

solidus, a, um, *adj.*, firm, sound.

sollemnis, e, *adj.*, stated, customary.

solum, ĭ, *n.*, the ground, soil.

solvō, solvī, solūtum (3), release, set free.

sōlus, a, um, *adj.*, alone (*gen.* sōlīus, *dat.* sōlī).

somnus, ĭ, *m.*, sleep.

sonitus, ūs, *m.*, noise; crash, l. 466.

sonō, uĭ (*no sup.*) (1), to sound.

sonus, ĭ, *m.*, a sound.

sopor, ōris, *m.*, sleep, slumber.

sors, tis, *f.*, lot, fate.

sortior, sortītus sum (4), choose out, select, by lot.

spargō, sĭ, sum (3), spread about, scatter.

Sparta, ae, *f.*, chief city of Laconia (Southern Greece).

speciēs, ēĭ, *f.*, sight, appearance.

spērō, āvī, ātum (1), hope for, expect.

spēs, eĭ, *f.*, hope.

spīra, ae, *f.*, a fold, a coil (*of a serpent*).

spissus, a, um, *adj.*, thick.

spolium, iĭ, *n.*, spoil, booty.

spōnsa, ae, *f.*, bride.

spūmeus, a, um, *adj.*, foaming.

spūmō, āvī, ātum (1), foam.

squāleō, be rough *or* stiff.

squāmeus, a, um, *adj.*, scaly.

stabulum, ĭ, *n.*, stall.

statiō, ōnis, *f.*, roadstead, anchorage.

statuō, uĭ, ūtum (3), set up, construct.

stella, ae, *f.*, star.

sternō, strāvī, strātum (3), scatter, overthrow, lay low.

Sthenelus, ĭ, *m.*, Sthenelus, charioteer of Diomedes.

stō, stetĭ, statum (1), stand.

strīdō, dĭ (*no sup.*) (3), creak.

stringō, strīnxĭ, strictum (3), draw, unsheathe.

struō, ūxĭ, ūctum (3), build, contrive.

studium, iĭ, *n.*, inclination, desire.

stupeō, be amazed at.

stuppeus, a, um, *adj.*, made of tow.

suādeō, sĭ, sum (3), advise, recommend.

sub, *prep.* + *acc.* and *abl.*, under.

subeō, īvī *or* iĭ, itum, *inf.* subīre, go under, occur (*to one's mind*), follow; come up, ll. 216, 467.

subiciō, ere, iēcĭ, iectum. throw *or* place under.

subitō, *adv.*, suddenly.

subitus, a, um, *adj.*, sudden.

sublābor, lāpsus sum (3), slip away, glide down.

sublātus, a, um, *perf. part. pass.* of tollō.

subsistō, stitĭ, stitum (3), stand still, stop, halt.

succēdō, cessī, cessum (3), go below, draw near, approach, *with dat.*

successus, ūs, *m.*, success.

succurrō, currī, cursum (3), run up to, help, succour (+ *dat.*).

sūdō, āvī, ātum (1), sweat, perspire (*with abl.*, be drenched with).

sūdor, ōris, *m.*, sweat.

sufferō, sustulĭ, sublātum, *inf.* sufferre, to hold up, sustain.

sufficiō, ere, fēcī, fectum, suffuse, supply.

sulcus, ī, m., furrow, trail (*of a meteor*).

sulfur, uris, n., brimstone, sulphur.

sum, fuī, *inf.* **esse,** be ; (*with dat.,* est mihi domus, I have a house).

summum, ī, n., top, summit.

summus, a, um, highest, greatest ; last, l. 334.

sūmo, psī, ptum (3), take, exact.

super, (*adv.*) in addition to, moreover ; *prep.* +*acc.,* over, above, upon ; *with abl.,* concerning, respecting.

superbus, a, um, *adj.,* proud, gorgeous.

superī, ōrum, m. (*alternative form* **superūm**), the gods above.

superō, āvī, ātum (1), rise above, be above, survive (*with dat.,* l. 643) ; pass over, cross.

supersum, fuī, *inf.* **esse,** be over and above, remain, survive.

superus, a, um, *adj.,* on high.

supplex, icis, c., a suppliant.

suprēmum, adv., for the last time.

suprēmus, a, um, *adj. superl. of* **superus.**

surgō, surrēxī, surrēctum (3), rise.

suscito, āvī, ātum (1), stir up.

suspectus, a, um, *adj.,* suspected.

suspēnsus, a, um, *adj.,* in suspense.

suus, a, um, *poss. pron.,* his, her, its, their, (own).

T

tabulātum, ī, n., floor, story.

taceō, uī, itum (2), be silent.

tacitus, a, um, *adj.,* silent.

tāctus, ūs, m., touch.

tālis, e, *adj.,* of such a kind.

tam, adv., so, very.

tamen, adv., yet, nevertheless.

tandem, adv., at length.

tantum, adv., so much, only.

tantus, a, um, *adj.,* so great.

tardus, a, um, *adj.,* slow.

taurus, ī, m., a bull.

tēctum, ī, n., roof, dwelling.

tēcum = cum tē.

tegō, tēxī, tēctum (3), cover, hide, protect.

tellūs, ūris, f., earth, land, country.

tēlum, ī, n., weapon, dart.

temperō, āvī, ātum (1), refrain, abstain.

tempestās, ātis, f., storm, tempest.

templum, ī, n., temple.

tempus, oris, n., time, occasion ; *in plur.* temples (of the head).

tendō, tetendī, tēnsum *or* tentum (3), stretch out ; go, strive.

tenebrae, ārum, f. *plur.*, darkness.

Tenedos, ī, f., Tenedos, island in the Aegean Sea, about five English miles from the coast of Troy.

teneō, uī, tum (2), hold, keep ; hold a position.

tener, era, erum, *adj.,* tender.

tentō, āvī, ātum (1), try, test, attempt.

tenuis, e, *adj.,* thin.

tenus, *prep.*, as far as (*gov. abl.
and follows the noun*).

ter, *num. adv.*, thrice.

terebrō, āvī, ātum (1), perforate,
bore through.

tergum, ī, *n.*, back.

terra, ae, *f.*, earth, ground, soil.

terreō, uī, itum (2), frighten.

testor, ātus sum (1), call to witness, invoke.

testūdō, inis, *f.*, a shell, tortoise;
(also a name given to a body
of soldiers advancing with
their shields held above their
heads, so as to lap over, like
the shell of a tortoise).

Teucrī, ōrum *or* Teucrum, *m.*,
Trojans—sprung from Teucer.

Teucria, ae, *f.*, Troy.

Teucrus, -a, -um, Trojan.

texō, uī, tum (3), weave, interlace.

thalamus, ī, *m.*, chamber.

Thessandrus, ī, *m.*, Thessandrus,
Greek leader, concealed in the
wooden horse.

Thoās, antis, *m.*, Thoas, Greek
hero.

Thybris, is, *m.*, Tiber, river of
Italy, flowing through Rome.

Thymoetēs, ae, *m.*, Thymoetes,
the Trojan who first suggested
that the wooden horse should
be brought into Troy.

timeō, uī (*no sup.*) (2), fear.

tollō, sustulī, sublātum (3), lift
up, raise.

torrēns, entis, *m.*, torrent.

torus, ī, *m.*, couch.

tot, *num. adj. indecl.*, so many.

totiēs, *num. adv.*, so many
times, so often.

tōtus, a, um, the whole.

trabs, is, *f.*, a beam.

trahō, trāxī, tractum (3), draw
or drag along ; lead, l. 457.

trāiciō, ere, iēcī, iectum, pierce.

tranquillus, a, um, *adj.*, calm,
quiet.

trānsferō, tulī, lātum, *inf.* ferre,
carry across.

tremefaciō, ere, fēcī, factum,
make to tremble.

tremendus, a, um, *gerundive of*
tremō, terrible.

tremō, uī (*no sup.*) (3), tremble,
quiver.

tremor, ōris, *m.*, trembling.

trepidō, āvī, ātum (1), tremble
with alarm, be in a state of
trepidation.

trepidus, a, um, *adj.*, trembling,
alarmed.

tridēns, entis, *m.*, three-pronged
spear, trident.

trīstis, e, *adj.*, sad.

trisulcus, a, um, *adj.*, having
three furrows, three-forked.

Trītōnis, idis *or* idos, *f.*, daughter
of Triton, i.e. Pallas.

Trītōnius, a, um, *adj.*, belonging
to Tritonia, i.e. Pallas.

triumphus, ī, *m.*, triumphal procession, triumph.

Trōes, um, *m.*, Trojans.

Trōia, ae, *f.*, Troy.

Trōiānus, a, um, *adj.*, Trojan.

Trōius, a, um, *adj.*, Trojan.

trucīdō, āvī, ātum (1), kill,
slaughter.

truncus, ī, *m.*, trunk (*of a tree*) ;
headless corpse.

tū, tuī, *pers. pron.* thou (*plur.*
vōs, *gen.* vestrūm *or* ī).

tuba, ae, *f.*, trumpet.

tueor, tuitus sum, (2), look upon, behold ; protect.

tum, *adv.*, then.

tŭmeō, (2), swell.

tumidus, a, um, *adj.*, swelling, swollen.

tumultus, ūs, *m.*, tumult, uproar.

tumulus, ī, *m.*, mound.

tunc, *adv.*, then.

turba, ae, *f.*, crowd.

turbō, āvī, ātum (1), agitate, disturb.

turbō, inis, *m.*, whirlwind, hurricane.

turpis, e, *adj.*, disgraceful, base.

turris, is, *f.*, tower (*acc.* turrim).

tūtor, tūtātus sum, (1), make safe, protect, defend.

tūtus, a, um, *adj.*, safe.

tuus, a, um, *poss. pron.*, thy, thine.

Tȳdidēs, ae, *m.*, son of Tydeus, i.e. Diomedes.

Tyndaris, idis, *f.*, daughter of Tyndareus, i.e. Helen.

U

ubi, *adv.*, when, where.

ubīque, *adv.*, everywhere, ll. 368, 369.

Ūcalegōn, ntis, *m.*, Ucalegon, a Trojan.

ulciscor, ultus sum, (3), avenge.

Ulixēs, ixī, *m.*, Ulysses, King of Ithaca, noted for his subtlety.

ūllus, a, um, *adj.*, any (*gen.* ūllīus, *dat.* ūllī).

ultimus, a, um, *adj.*, last (*superl.*

of a *comparative* ulterior, akin to ultrā).

ultor, ōris, *m.*, avenger.

ultrīx, trīcis, *adj.*, avenging.

ultrō, *adv.*, of one's own accord, voluntarily.

ululō, āvī, ātum (1), to howl.

ulva, ae, *f.*, sedge.

umbō, ōnis, *m.*, boss of a shield, shield.

umbra, ae, *f.*, shade, shadow, ghost.

umerus, ī, *m.*, shoulder.

ūmidus, a, um, *adj.*, damp, dank.

umquam, *adv.*, ever, at any time.

ūnā, *adv.*, at one and the same time, together.

unda, ae, *f.*, wave, water.

unde, *adv.*, whence.

undique, *adv.*, on all sides.

undō, āvī, ātum (1), rise in waves, surge.

ūnus, a, um, *adj.*, alone, only, one (*gen.* ūnius *or* ūnīus, *dat.* ūnī).

urbs, bis, *f.*, city.

urgeō, ursī (*no sup.*) (2), press hard, be urgent.

ūrō, ussī, ūstum (3), burn.

usquam, *adv.*, anywhere.

usque, *adv.*, continually, constantly.

ūsus, ūs, *m.*, use, employment.

ut, when, as, how, as soon as ; that, in order that.

uterque, utraque, utrumque, *pron. and adj.*, each, both (*gen.* utrīusque, *dat.* utrīque).

uterus, ī, *m.*, belly.

utinam, *adv.*, oh that, would that.

V

vacuus, a, um, *adj.*, empty, un-
occupied.

vādō (*no perf. or sup.*) (3), go.

vagor, ātus sum, (1), wander,
circulate widely (*of a report*).

valeō, ūi, itum (2), be strong,
be able, avail; *imperative*
valē, farewell.

validus, a, um, *adj.*, strong,
mighty.

vallis, is, *f.*, a valley.

vānus, a, um, *adj.*, vain, idle,
false.

varius, a, um, *adj.*, various, different.

vāstus, a, um, *adj.*, immense.

vātēs, is, *c.*, soothsayer.

vel, *conj.*, or.

velim, *pres. subj.* of volō.

vellō, vellī, vulsum (3), pluck *or*
tear away.

vēlo, āvī, ātum (1), cover.

vēlum, ī, *n.*, sail, covering.

velutī, *adv.*, even as, just as.

venēnum, ī, *n.*, poison.

veniō, vēnī, ventum (4), come.

venter, tris, *m.*, belly.

ventus, ī, *m.*, wind.

verbum, ī, *n.*, word.

vērō, *adv.*, indeed.

vērum, *adv.*, truly, even so, but.

versō, āvī, ātum (1), turn over,
ponder.

vertō, ī, sum, (3), turn ; overthrow, l. 625.

vertex, icis, *m.*, top *or* crown (*of
the head*), summit (*of a thing*).

vērus, a, um, *adj.*, true ; *neut.*
as noun, truth (l. 141).

Vesta, ae, *f.*, Vesta, goddess of
the hearth.

vester, tra, trum, *poss. pron.*,
your.

vestibulum, ī, *n.*, porch, vesti-
bule.

vestis, is, *f.*, garment.

vestīgium, iī, *n.*, footprint ;
step.

veterrimus, a, um, *adj. superl. of*
vetus.

vetus, eris, *adj.*, old, ancient.

vetustus, a, um, *adj.*, ancient.

via, ae, *f.*, way, course.

vibrō, āvī, ātum (1), flicker.

vicis, *acc.* vicem, *abl.* vice (*plur.*
vicēs, *abl.* vicibus, *other cases
wanting*), change, vicissitude.

victor, tōris, *m.*, conqueror (*as
an adj.*, victorious).

victōria, ae, *f.*, victory.

victus, a, um, *perf. part. pass. of*
vinco.

videndus, a, um, *gerundive of*
videō.

videō, vīdī, vīsum (2), see, *pass.*
videor, appear (*impers.*, vīsum
est, it seemed good).

vigeō (*no perf. or sup.*) (2),
flourish.

vigil, *adj.*, wakeful, on the
watch.

vigil, is, *m.*, sentinel.

vinculum *or* vinclum, ī, *n.*,
chain, bond, fetter.

vincō, vīcī, victum (3), conquer.

vīnum, ī, *n.*, wine.

violābilis, e, *adj.*, that may be
violated, violable.

violō, āvī, ātum (1), force, violate.

vir, virī, *m.*, man.

virgineus, a, um, *adj.*, belonging
to a virgin ; maiden.

virgō, inis, *f.*, maiden, virgin.
virtūs, ūtis, *f.*, valour, bravery, virtue.
vīs, *acc.* vim, *abl.* vī, *f.* (*plur.* vīrēs, *gen.* vīrium, *abl.* vīribus), force, strength.
vīsō, sī (*no sup.*) (3), look attentively at, go to see.
vīsus, a, um, *perf. partic. pass.* of vídeō.
vīsus, ūs, *m.*, sight, vision.
vīta, ae, *f.*, life.
vītō, āvī, ātum (1), avoid, shun.
vitta, ae, *f.*, band, fillet, garland.
vīvus, a, um, living, running (*of a stream*).
vix, *adv.*, scarcely, with difficulty.
vōciferāns, tis, *pres. part.* of

vōciferor, ātus sum (1), cry out.
vocō, āvī, ātum (1), call, summon.
volō, voluī, *inf.* velle, wish, desire.
volucer, cris, cre, *adj.*, swift, fleeting.
volūmen, inis, *n.*, fold, coil.
volvō, vī, ūtum (3), roll.
vōtum, ī, *n.*, vow, votive offering.
vōx, vōcis, *f.*, voice, word, saying.
Vulcānus, ī, *m.*, Vulcan, the fire-god.
vulgus, ī, *n.*, the common people.
vulnus, eris, *n.*, wound.
vultus, ūs, *m.*, face, countenance.

Zephyrus, ī, *m.*, west wind.

ADDENDA

adverto, -ere, -tī, -sum (3), heed, (712).
amnis, -is, *m.*, river.
artus, -ūs, *m.*, limb.
fātus, *see* for.
latus, -eris, *n.*, side.
pāstor, -ōris, *m.*, shepherd.
quisque, quidque, each.
quōcumque, *adv.*, whithersoever; howsoever, (709).